MEMORY AND L

CW00666458

Memory is a major factor in the composition
research into how the brain and memory functiν.. ┌-
can best meet the needs of worshippers.

In *Memory and Liturgy*, Peter Atkins draws on the fruits of his research into the
process of the brain and our memory and applies it to liturgical worship. His
extensive experience in writing and using liturgy keeps this book rooted in reality.
In its ten chapters the author applies the functioning of the brain and the memory
to our remembrance of God in worship; God's memory of us through Baptism; our
remembrance of Jesus Christ in the Eucharist; the corporate memory of the
community created through worship; the healing of memories of sin and pain
through forgiveness; three aids to help us worship; the process of continuity and
change in liturgy; and the connection between memory, imagination and hope.

The conclusion summarizes the main practical issues. This provides a check-list
for those serving on Liturgical Commissions and those involved in the teaching of
the practice of liturgy. This book is a positive contribution to the ongoing search
for suitable liturgical worship and music for the twenty-first century.

In memory
of all those saints and colleagues
who have inspired me
with the words and drama
of liturgical worship

Memory and Liturgy

The Place of Memory in the Composition and Practice of Liturgy

PETER ATKINS
*Retired Anglican Bishop and former Lecturer
in Theology, University of Auckland*

ASHGATE

Published by
Ashgate Publishing Limited
Gower House, Croft Road
Aldershot, Hants
GU11 3HR
England

Ashgate Publishing Company
Suite 420
101 Cherry Street
Brookfield VT 05401–4405
USA

Ashgate website: http://www.ashgate.com

British Library Cataloguing in Publication Data
Atkins, Peter, 1936–
    Memory and liturgy : the place of memory in the composition
    and practice of liturgy
    1. Memory–Religious aspects 2. Public worship–
    Christianity–Psychological aspects
    Title
    264'.0019

Library of Congress Cataloging-in-Publication Data
Atkins, Peter, 1936–
    Memory and liturgy : the place of memory in the composition
    and practice of liturgy / Peter Atkins.
        p. cm.
    Includes bibliographical references and index.
    1. Liturgics. I. Title.
    BV176.3.A85 2003
    264'.001'9–dc21

                                                                        2003044388

ISBN 0 7546 0869 7 (Hbk)
ISBN 0 7546 0870 0 (Pbk)

This book is printed on acid-free paper

Typeset in Times Roman by SetSystems Ltd, Saffron Walden, Essex

Printed and bound in Great Britain by MPG Books Ltd, Bodmin, Cornwall

Contents

Acknowledgements

My love of liturgy was first inspired by Dean Dwelly at Liverpool Cathedral in the 1950s. He had an exact eye for colour and movement and so was able to match the grandeur of the emerging building with the activity of the human actors in the drama of the divine liturgy. A greater appreciation of liturgy grew through the new developments in the celebration of the Eucharist put in place by John Robinson as dean of Clare College in Cambridge in the latter part of the same decade. In the 1960s my inspiration came from the new prayer book for the Province of Melanesia in the Pacific which was devised by Canon Charles Fox, one of its honoured linguists and saints. Soon after my return to New Zealand I was invited to join the Commission set up there to revise the services for the Anglican Church of that Province. I shared that task for the next 17 years. It was a privilege to be part of that multi-talented team so inclusive of age, gender, culture, language and church order. *A New Zealand Prayer Book/He Karakia Mihinare o Aotearoa*[1] was published for Advent 1989, and twelve months later I was teaching Liturgy and Worship as part of the degree course at St John's College in Auckland, again in an ecumenical team situation. The regular inspiration for my worship came from a daily and weekly pattern of services in parish, diocesan and college settings. To all of these 'saints' who helped to develop my relationship to God through worship I acknowledge a deep debt of gratitude.

As I record this list, a host of vivid memories is evoked, rich and powerful in their association with people, places and prayer. It was a few years ago when I wrote and gathered the material for *Worship 2000! – Resources to celebrate the new millennium*[2] that I began to make the connection between memory and liturgy. I wanted to find out how our brains create the memories which bring to mind the wonderful experiences of God in worship – both for the individual and for the corporate body of Christ. I also wanted to understand more fully why some people resisted the new words for worship, and declared that we were trampling on sacred memories. Those questions so teased my brain that I knew that I needed help to discover the answers. My years on the Faculty of Theology at the University of Auckland encouraged me to take advantage of their interdisciplinary approach to learning. Through the dean of Theology I was put in touch with the deans of the Schools of Medicine and of Education. Respectively they found for me two colleagues for this journey of discovery.

Dr Roger Booth undertakes teaching and research in the area of brain function within the department of Molecular Medicine. I warmly acknowledge Roger's patience and guidance as I read the literature, watched the videos he lent me, and with him attended a series of Robb lectures at the University given by Professor

---

[1] First published by Collins, and referred to as NZPB (1989) in this work.
[2] Peter Atkins (1999), *Worship 2000! – Resources to celebrate the new millennium*.

Steven Pinker from the Massachusetts Institute of Technology.[3] Dr Booth helped me to find the words to describe the working of the brain and the memory function, and then apply these findings to my own field of liturgy. Of course what I have written is my own, but I acknowledge Dr Booth's quiet expertise in pointing me in the right direction.

For Chapter 7 of this book, 'Memories of Sin and Pain', I needed to have access to any research into ways to 'correct' memory patterns laid in the brain as a result of misinterpretation of data or from false learning. Dr Richard Hamilton of the Research Centre for Interventions in Teaching and Learning made available to me the summaries of research printed in journals which set out ways to correct mis-learnt or mistaken concepts in the fields of science. I acknowledge with gratitude the way Richard so quickly realized the issues I was raising and provided me with the photocopies of the relevant research. Dr Hamilton also read my draft material and gave me useful comments. I was fortunate for this chapter that I had access to Dr Charles Elliott's outstanding research[4] into the connection between memory and the theology of salvation which helped me to fill in the gaps in my understanding of the way the brain can undertake the process of accepting forgiveness. Again the words in Chapter 7 are mine, but the research comes from specialists in a wider field.

In retirement I am so fortunate to have the resources of a first-rate theological library near my home. I acknowledge the help of Mrs Judith Bright and the staff at the library of the College of St John the Evangelist, Auckland, both in locating material and also letting me borrow armfuls of books for a month at a time. My own liturgical library has been enlarged during the last six years as I have had the privilege to review a number of recent books in this specialist area. As a regular contributor to *Reviews in Religion and Theology*[5] I am grateful to its editor, Dr Isabel Wollaston, for selecting such books for me to review.

The proposal for this book was submitted to Sarah Lloyd, publisher at Ashgate Publishing Ltd of Aldershot in May 2001. I was very grateful for her enthusiasm and for the advice of her series editors for Liturgy, Worship and Society. In their wisdom they encouraged me to widen the research and take 18 months for the writing process. This has indeed given me the chance to explore issues at greater depth, and also maintain my other writing programmes. I acknowledge the value of this advice and the care they have taken to bring this book to publication.

Finally I pay tribute once again to the constant support of my wife Rosemary, who so patiently debates with me the flow of enthusiastic ideas I pour forth and thus helps me to mature them into more worthy offerings for a wider audience. Like me she shares a passion for good liturgy.

To all these friends, living and departed, I acknowledge my indebtedness, and give thanks to God for the way liturgy has been sustained as a living and memorable activity within the whole Body of Christ.

Auckland, New Zealand   All Saints' Day 2002

---

[3] See Steven Pinker (1999), *How the mind works.*
[4] Elliott Charles (1995), *Memory and Salvation.*
[5] Published by Blackwell, Oxford, five times a year.

Introduction

Curiosity

Curiosity is a very human attribute, and curiosity is to be largely credited for the germ of the idea that in the end gave rise to this book. I had heard about the current research into the working of the brain. At the same time I was saddened by the difficulties experienced by a number of friends who were suffering from a severe loss of memory. My curiosity was aroused as to what the new research had to tell us about the way the brain worked. In particular I was eager to know what caused the memory to function, and why and how it could lose its ability to 'remember'. This basic curiosity was extended when I realized what an important place my own memories had in my approach to the composition and practice of liturgy. How did my brain cope with continuity and change? Why was I angry when a hymn was sung to a different tune to the one I remembered and with which I had many positive associations? So the ideas for *Memory and Liturgy* were born from basic curiosity. That is a curiosity that I trust those engaged in the composition and practice of liturgy will share. As they follow the findings of the research, my hope is that they will discover how liturgy can fulfill its objective of enhancing our relationship with God and keeping the nature and presence of God in the forefront of our minds.

Two Commands in the Liturgy

There are two key phrases in the liturgy of the Eucharist which hold strong memories for me. The first is part of the 'Summary of the Law' which in the New Zealand Prayer Book liturgy often precedes the invitation to confession:

> Hear the teaching of Christ:
> you shall love the Lord your God
> . . . with all your mind.[1]

The second comes later in the same liturgy during the Great Thanksgiving Prayer:

> Take, eat, this is my body
> which is given for you;
> do this to remember me.

---

[1]   NZPB (1989), p. 406.

> After supper he took the cup;
> . . . do this as often as you drink it,
> to remember me.[2]

Love God with all Your Mind

On hearing these words and knowing of the current research I asked how I could really love God with all my mind if I did not know what my mind did and how it worked. What was the connection between my mind and my brain? Now that modern scientific discovery was revealing the working of the brain, could the brain also be regarded as the seat of the emotions (the heart in Biblical terms), and of our religious capacity to respond to God (the soul in Biblical terms)? I had heard about the theory that there were right and left sides to the brain – one governing a person's feelings and the other one's logical processes, though that is far too simple an explanation of both the research and the findings as I was to discover as I wrote this book. My interest in the Myers Briggs personality preference theory has developed as I have shared with Professor Leslie Francis the task of writing a series of Gospel commentaries in the *Personality Type and Scripture* series.[3] I wanted to discover how that theory might be connected to the functioning of the brain. So the command to love God with all my mind stimulated my quest for knowledge.

Do This to Remember Me

In my teaching of liturgy and worship as part of my duties as a lecturer in theology in the University of Auckland I had become more and more interested in the meaning of the word 'remember' when it was used in the Great Thanksgiving Prayer. I considered that if I could really come to grips with what this word meant I could begin to sort out the various positions taken in the sharp debate about the way in which Christ could be said to be present during the Eucharist. My elementary grasp of the Hebrew language has taught me that the best way to understand words in another language is to see the context in which they are used on various occasions, and also the associated ideas that are linked to those words. When I was engaged in the current research I realized that 'linkage' and 'association' (or reference as it is also called) is a basic feature of memory. So this book has helped me to see the word 'to remember' in two new ways:

1   'To remember' can be causative, that is, this object or idea will cause you to remember that one.

---

[2] NZPB (1989), p. 422.
[3] Published by Mowbray/Continuum with the titles: *Exploring Luke's Gospel* (2000); *Exploring Matthew's Gospel* (2001); *Exploring Mark's Gospel – Revised and expanded edition* (2002).

2   'To remember' is to link past, present and future in a single fold. The brain has
this fantastic capacity to work in a multi-time zone without loosing touch (if it
is functioning 'normally') with the reality of time. I can make the past present,
and I can imagine the future now, while at the same time remaining aware of
the 'history' of the past, and the 'image' of the future. The brain does not
operate on the 'either-or' principle, but has a 'both-and' ability.

So in the liturgy the call 'to remember' at the time of thanksgiving for the bread
and the wine at the Eucharist can *cause* the brain to recall the presence of Christ
for this moment of time while also recognizing that Jesus is part of history and that
his presence now foreshadows the coming again of Christ in future glory. So I
approached the writing of Chapter 5 of this book with a new set of insights.

Seeing Inside My Head

I began the exciting journey of discovery through research for this book with that
eerie feeling of looking at my inner self from an outside position. I knew I had to
learn to think about the very activity of thinking. I had to see inside my head and
observe the very pattern of thoughts about which I was thinking. I became aware
that much of the research into the brain had taken place in the last fifty years.
When I asked 'why?' the response was a sobering one. Until we had modern
scanning machines it was only possible to observe the brains of those who were
dead, when the brain had ceased to function. In the last fifty years it has become
possible to observe (though still with some difficulty) the workings of the living
brain. Such research is still a guessing game where the researcher must fill in the
gaps to make deductions from what has been observed. But then the 'guessing
game' is exactly what the brain has been set up to play, and it is remarkably adept
at guessing and testing the appropriate answers.

To undertake the research of seeing inside my head I had the good fortune to
meet Dr Roger Booth of the School of Medicine at the University of Auckland.
His generosity I have already acknowledged on page vii. With his help I was able
to write the first two chapters of this book. Originally I thought that I could cover
the functioning of the brain and the memory in one chapter, but I quickly realized
that these were two different topics and that each had major implications for the
composition and practice of liturgy.

The Brain at Work

Chapter 1 records what I discovered about the way the brain works. I was humbled
by what I learnt and fell in awe 'at the feet of my Creator'. Humanity is indeed
'wonderfully made'. In our brains we have a truly amazing instrument not only for
gathering information but also for computing it so that we can act on what we have
received. The immensity of its design and its capabilities still leaves me with a
sense of mystery. In addition it is the instrument that allows us to be in touch with
the divine Creator. It is the home of the spirit which can link us to the Divine

Spirit – and this makes worship and relationship possible. Sir Charles Sherrington speaks of a 'cosmic dance' which occurs in the brain.[4] For me this became a parable of the great cosmic dance in which my spirit engages every time I take part in worship. On those occasions I link with worshippers present in person and present in memory and in imagination, and join the 'dance' of adoration and praise to the Triune God within whose nature is the ultimate dance of love and wholeness.[5]

I conclude the first chapter with some initial thoughts on the implications of this research for liturgical worship. Other implications keep occurring throughout the book, and so I have decided that these should be gathered together in summary form in a Conclusion.

How the Memory Works

Because the focus in this book is primarily on the memory function, Chapter 2 is devoted to a greater understanding of how our memory works. As what we know is closely tied to what we remember, this chapter is as much about knowledge as it is about memory. Before my research I had not realized that we imitate to learn and learn to imitate from the cradle to the grave. This puts a responsibility on each generation to 'model' the art and practice of worship for the next generation. Worship cannot survive as an activity for individuals. It is a corporate art and a corporate responsibility. This observation and some guidance from the series editors at Ashgate Publishing caused me to add a chapter on corporate memory (Chapter 6) to my first proposal for the contents of the book.

We can only know who we are if we remember to whom we are related. This is a sober reminder to a society that tries to glorify the individual to the point that individuals are encouraged to think that they can cast themselves adrift from the community as a whole. The way our memory accumulates knowledge tells us this is nonsense, and dangerous nonsense at that.

---

[4] See Chapter 1, page 5.
[5] This is well expressed in the final verse of a hymn by Marie Barrell, one of New Zealand's many composers:

> Great and deep the Spirit's purpose,
> nothing shall be left to chance.
> All the lives will be united
> in the everlasting dance.
> All fulfilled and all perfected,
> each uniquely loved and known,
> Christ in glory unimagined
> once for all receives his own.

By 'unimagined' I assume she means 'on the edge of our imagination', for what we cannot imagine does not register in the mental process. (See Chapter 10.)

Remembering God

Once I enter into worship I remember who I am and to whom I am related. The basis of worship is the relationship between us and God, and this relationship is re-enacted and further developed every time we remember God. The advantage of the way our brains are designed is that they can hold together a vast array of memories and knowledge so that we can integrate a substantial picture of the nature of the Almighty. The regular repetition of the knowledge about God allows the worshipper to hold on to the great variety of such knowledge. The tendency in modern liturgy is to multiply alternatives in the forms of prayer and to simplify theology. Liturgy, because it is frightened of being boring to the worshipper, provides much variety in expressing the one simplified theological statement 'God is love'. The account of the many-sided nature of God often becomes shortened. The temptation in worship has been to reduce the number and length of the Scripture readings and frequently to omit the full statements of the belief of the Church as expressed in one of the Creeds. Thus the worshipper, who is capable of integrating a multifaceted presentation of the nature of God, is presented with a trimmed-down theology within the liturgy. Our brains call out to be used more extensively and become dissatisfied with the limited opportunity to remember God in all God's fullness.

Baptism – God's Remembrance of Us

The sacrament of Baptism has been a cause of division as well as unity for Christians. Baptism has been widely accepted as the means of entry into the whole Christian community, but how baptism should be administered and to whom, has been the subject of deep divisions. If we approach this sacrament as the assurance of God's memory of us, a whole new dimension emerges. In Chapter 4 we will see how the brain is capable of constantly updating the relationship with God established at baptism. We remember who we are because of what God has done for humanity. Our own very name recalls both our birth and our new birth in Christ at baptism. In this chapter I examine in turn five metaphors for baptism and show how memory is vital to the way we can bring these metaphors to life. Such life can only remain current as the memories are reactivated through regular worship. One of the key reasons for worship is to prevent spiritual amnesia – the loss of memory as to who we are and who God is. The connection between baptism and worship therefore needs to be frequently re-presented in our liturgy, and I have outlined ways in which this might be done.

Remembering Jesus Christ

In the heart of the book, in Chapter 5, I examine the central topic of how we remember Jesus Christ. I aim to show how research into the functioning of the brain helps us to see how our memory of Jesus Christ is enabled through reinterpretation and re-enactment. The sacrament of the Eucharist provides us with all the necessary 'triggers' for this memory to stay active. First of all the 'memory' is evoked through Scripture as it is read in the fellowship of the Church. Then the 'memory' is re-enacted through the spirit of prayer and the communion of contemplation. In particular worshippers find the memory of Jesus Christ, the Risen and Ascended Lord, comes into sharp focus at the Eucharistic Table. So in this chapter I discuss the ways that our brains are capable of interpreting 'presence' and provide us with new insights into what Jesus might have meant by his words 'Do this to remember me'. When we examine the various parts of the Liturgy of the Eucharist in detail we can see how memory provides the means for the worshippers to recall the person and presence of Christ, both as Saviour and Lord.

Corporate Memory

The person of Christ, Christ's body, and the body of the Church, are all so linked through our memory at the Eucharist that our brains tell us that each individual is forever linked with the corporate whole. I was particularly conscious of this corporate aspect of our lives when in mid-2000 I was asked to provide the sermon for a Commemoration service at my Cambridge college.[6] A group of alumni from the late 1950s were gathered to assist the college celebrate the generosity of its leading scholars and benefactors from the time of its foundation more than four hundred years earlier. This corporate memory still inspires its current vibrant community of scholars as they face the changing circumstances of today's world. Their tradition is sustained by the best of the past as it is adapted to meet the challenges of the present context. At the same time they must amend the tradition of learning to meet the emerging, just imagined, circumstances of the future. Out of its memory it forms its continuing identity and passes on its evolving story to the next generation. As always with the gathering of alumni (and now also alumnae) there is a temptation towards nostalgia, but if we allow our brains to function properly, they allow us to stay firmly rooted in the reality of the present situation. As the two generations of scholars meet, many hopes are expressed about the future health and effectiveness of the ongoing community. Memory and imagination combine to make certain that the future is at least equal to the past.

As I shared the sermon in the College chapel I was conscious of the heavy responsibility that rests with each generation to keep the 'tradition' in these memories alive. Once the tradition has been lost the bonds with the past and the hopes for the future are broken. Equally society as a whole is in danger of losing so many important memories – particularly in the area of corporate worship. The Church needs to consider afresh its responsibility to remind society of its need for corporate worship, and to find ways to reach out to the wider community before it loses the art of functioning as a worshipping body. I took my experience at my own college into account as I wrote the material for Chapter 6 and looked at the connection between worship and the maintenance of corporate memory. This

---

[6] Commemoration of Benefactors at Sidney Sussex College, Cambridge, 1 July 2000.

chapter ends with an examination of the opportunities provided to the community to celebrate the 'rites of passage' with appropriate liturgy.

Healing Memories of Guilt and Pain

The healing of painful memories has been a focus of attention in society as we become even more aware of the hurts that have been afflicted on so many of our community. Chapter 7 examines whether it is possible for the brain and memory function to erase or let go such painful memories in such a way that the outcome is positive for the health of the individual and of society. I was fortunate in being able to access some key research in the field of science education through the good offices of Dr Richard Hamilton of the Department of Education at the University of Auckland. I aimed to apply this to the field of liturgy, and I found many key areas where the research was very useful. Charles Elliott's book *Memory and Salvation*[7] also helped me to see some of the implications in relation to sin and forgiveness. In particular I am convinced that the brain has the ability to re-weight the significance of a memory by laying alongside the memory of hurt and guilt the more powerful memory of salvation and forgiveness. Christians exercise such reworking of significance every Good Friday when the cross, the symbol of shame, becomes the cross of glorious redemption. At the conclusion of Chapter 7 I examine the role of liturgy in bringing about the mending of a memory, while still retaining the memory of the consequences of sin that are so hurtful to the individual and the community. Again the brain is capable of this both-and conjunction, even when the joy of healing and the pain of hurt are found in such contrary memories.

Aids to Remembrance

I am by birth an Irishman, and so I have always valued a sense of holy space, symbol and time. Anyone who has had the opportunity to stand beneath one of the towering carved high crosses of the Celtic Church will know of its sense of the sacred. Such crosses – made first in wood and then in stone – marked the places where the itinerant missionary monks would stand and proclaim the Christian gospel. The carvings on the cross retold the story of God's people and became an aid to remembrance for those who heard the story for the first time. Later generations raised a church building near to those already holy places to house the faithful and to give them a continuing memory of the holiness of God. There the worshippers would find a sense of awe and mystery, and learn to develop their relationship with God. The same God would also go before them to every hill and valley, and across the seas to the furthest continents and islands of the globe. Such missionaries in turn would carry with them the symbols of the sacred to recall their memory of the continuing presence of God in Word and Sacrament.

In Chapter 8 I examine the power of such spaces and symbols to evoke our

---

[7] Elliott, Charles (1995).

remembrance of God. At the same time the way that the brain operates makes us realize that spaces and symbols can become sterile if the memory of the community is unable to maintain reference and links to the reality to which these point. The Church has also used 'time' as another aid to remembering who God is and what God has done. The annual calendar is a key instrument by which both Church and society 'remembers' the Christian story, and stays in touch with its power to transform lives.

Continuity and Change

As one of those involved for many years in the revision of liturgy and the composition of new liturgical material I was fascinated by the reaction – both in myself and in others – to the issues of continuity and change. I have delivered, and suffered, tirades on the topic and have always wondered what were the factors involved in such reactions. In Chapter 9 I set out the fruits of my research, and also of some of my experience. I now more fully realize why some people had such varying responses to 'new' forms of liturgy. Much of the enthusiasm and the bitterness could have been better understood if we had spent some more time in examining the factors in continuity and change, even if this meant a little less time for the contents of the proposed liturgies.

What was true about liturgy in general, was, and still is, true about continuity and change in music, as every congregation and its musicians know only too well. In the last twenty years there has been a crescendo of new music within worship, and this has led to both excitement and confusion. Brian Wren in *Praying Twice*[8] has provided us with much good advice and comment on the way that we might handle the opportunities for new music without disregarding our treasured memories of music from a previous generation. He and I both point to the value of tradition without losing our enthusiasm for contemporary words and music.

Memory, Imagination and Hope

In Chapter 10 I look at the connection between memory, imagination and hope. The imaginative function is a key part of the brain's work. Without it we could not be in touch with the Divine or see ourselves beyond the immediate situation in which we live. Using the available research I describe the nature of imagination and apply that to the way liturgy can exercise that function in relation to the Divine. Imagination is an essential component in the art of praying, both for ourselves and others. In Biblical terms there is a strong connection between the working of the Holy Spirit and the function of the imagination. This is not only true in prayer but also in the receipt of guidance for the future. For that future we are sustained by hope, a hope that imagination is able to foresee and foretaste, long before we can attain the future in reality.

---

[8]   Wren, Brian (2000).

Implications for the Composition and Practice of Liturgy

This journey of discovery has been a rewarding one for me personally because it has brought to light so much about the relationship I have with God through worship. My hope is that as I share the revelations of the research, so those responsible for the composition and practice of liturgy will be able to do this work with a greater understanding of the way our brains and our memory function operate. In the Conclusion I have tried, for ease of convenience, to summarize the practical issues that have arisen from this study. This should provide an easy reference document and also fulfill what has been so obvious from the research – that repetition and 'chunking' is essential if we are to retain what we have committed to memory.

Praise to God for 'Holy Brain'

It is right to give praise to God who gave us such a wonderful instrument in our brains to enrich our memories and our lives. With the brain I enter into my relationship with God in worship. With the brain I remember who I am, made a child of God and a member of the Church at baptism. With the brain I recall Christ's presence through the Word and Sacrament during the liturgy of the Eucharist. With the brain I share in the corporate memory of my community and keep alive the story of the Church. With the brain I balance the memory of my sin and guilt with the good news of my salvation through Jesus Christ. With the brain I can use space, symbol and time as aids to my remembrance of the holy. With the brain I can treasure continuity and adapt to change. With the brain my imagination can help me see over the horizon of my present knowledge to the glorious future of the fulfillment of God's purpose. With such a wonderful instrument I can remember all things, hope all things, and enjoy all the things that are in store for those who love God.

Praise be to God for 'holy brain'.

Chapter 1

Discovering How the Brain Works

Research during the twentieth century has allowed us to gain a good understanding of how our brain works.[1] Such discoveries give rise to a new terminology to describe what has been found, but fortunately for the general reader we can also draw on some parallel language from our common experience to help us interpret what is going on in our heads.

Under the Microscope

The human brain has some one million, million brain cells, which are called *neurons*. There are some cells other than neurons in the brain but these are not involved in the neurological system I am describing. Under a powerful microscope a neuron looks like a super-octopus[2] with a central body from which a multitude of arms or tentacles spread out. These tentacles have been likened to branches of a tree, spreading out from a series of trunks to tiny branches at the ends. These arms or branches have been given the name of *dendrites*, and the main trunk has been called the *axon*.[3] It is the axon which carries 'information' from the neuron through its dendrites.

At the edge of each dendrite (branch) there are little spine-like features or buttons and it is these which contain chemicals which are the message carriers. These facilitate the thinking process as messages are circulated from one neuron to another. These spines or buttons act as receptors for 'information' passed on from the next neuron. They also act as the transmitters of 'information' from that neuron to the next brain cell. The amount of 'information' circulating is vast and everything happens simultaneously. Each cell could be said to have the capacity to act like a giant telephone exchange, receiving signals and sending out messages – and all this happens in the brain in microseconds.[4]

---

[1] Refer to the bibliography for some of the fruits of this research, in particular Pinker, Steven (1999), *How the Mind Works*; Buzan, Tony (1993), *The Mind Map Book*; Buzan, Tony (1995), *Use Your Head* and Calvin, William (1997), *How Brains Think: Evolving Intelligence, Then and Now*.

[2] For a picture of the brain see Buzan (1993), p. 31.

[3] Buzan (1993), p. 27 defines dendrites and axon in this way: 'The branches of the brain cell are called dendrites (defined as "natural tree-like markings or structures"). One particular and long branch, called the axon, is the main exit for information transmitted by that cell.'

[4] Compare Buzan (1993), p. 29.

The Causes of 'Information' Circulation

That then is the general picture. We can now ask the obvious question: what causes the 'information' to flow? There are a number of causes. One cause may be a stimulus received from one or more of the receptors in the body – the ear for sound, the nose for smell, the mouth for taste, and the skin for touch. This 'information' is transmitted to the brain which circulates it for interpretation, reaction and storage. On the other hand the brain itself might cause the 'information' to flow. We say: 'I had a thought.' This 'information' arises from energy within the brain itself, and not from an external stimulus. Such 'information' is also circulated between neurons so that the thought is interpreted, evaluated and may cause a reaction triggering other 'information' to flow.

Thinking

So we have to ask 'What is thinking?' To be able to say that 'I have a thought about something' three conditions are required. First, I must be alive. Second, I must be a human being. Third, I must have a consciousness of 'self'; that is I must be able to differentiate between myself and other beings. So the art of thinking can only be carried out by a person who has the capacity to act and observe. Our thinking ability arises from our communal life in a mutual society. We quite literally 'learn to think'.

What then gives us the 'trigger' to be able to function on this action/reflection model? We start out as a newborn baby who has no need to 'think' about the basic actions for life. Any thinking has to be done for us, and our built-in responses allow us to carry on with the basics of life: breathing, eating, discharging, growing. Gradually, over the first four years of life, we begin to develop meaning from the sense information received through the eye and the touch, that is, from interaction with 'other'. Pleasure is associated with the mother through feeding *and* smiling. Patterns in the brain are established to provide information circuits and enable bodily functions. We begin to see ourselves as distinct to those we 'see' as other. As all parents know, the child begins to have a 'mind' of its own.

Our Mind

In this way it may be helpful to talk of our brain as if it were like a computer, and our mind as the facility we develop to give commands to the computer.[5] The brain,

---

[5] There seems to be some debate among the experts on the correlation between the mind and the brain. Pinker (1999) states: 'The mind is not the brain, but what the brain does, and not even everything it does, such as metabolizing fat or giving off heat' (p. 24). Earlier he says: 'The mind is a system of organs of computation designed by natural selection to solve the kinds of problems our ancestors faced in their ... way of life'

being a physical structure contained within a living human body, operates as a closed system in a totally deterministic manner. It is closed in the sense that it has no direct access to the world outside the human body. It therefore cannot operate with any representations of that world. Neurons only know about connections with other neurons. The changes that take place moment by moment in the brain are completely determined by the structure of the neuronal network and the messages from the sense organs which it receives at every moment. Patterns of connection and electrochemical activity from the ends of the dendrites become encoded in this network of operations. However the brain cannot of itself 'choose' patterns any more than my computer chooses what character to display on the screen. There must be a 'mind' which taps the key on the computer which then is able to pass on that message and act on it.

The mind makes the choices and decisions for the self-conscious person. It is the mind that recognizes the possibilities from the images of multiple patterns of past experience and of future possibilities and makes evaluation between the possibilities. It is the mind that reaches the decision and conveys this to the working brain.

Gerald Edelman, who received a Nobel Prize in 1993, has developed the theory[6] that the mind is that function of the brain in human beings which has the ability to make choices in reference to the observed world. This function could be said to be the result of 'natural selection' in the Darwinian sense. However this is not on a generation-to-generation basis but in the early growth phase of the unique individual that we are. The brain itself has processed natural selection in developing a function which selects from the inputs what enables it to carry out its work most effectively. This brain function, which Edelman located in some neurons deep in the cerebral cortex, gives a weighting of value or significance to what is processed by the brain. So it is that we make sense of what we observe by the weight of significance or value that this function places on the inputs in the brain system. These neurons send out signals which multiply or diminish the strength of the received 'information' being passed between the neurons. This sense of value is closely associated with feelings and emotions. What brings satisfaction and positive feelings to the individual, and to the relationship between the individual and the circle around him or her, is weighted as valuable or unimportant by this function of the brain. According to this theory this allows these cells in the brain to exercise 'choices' between the possibilities for action and behaviour. For the sake of distinction this function has been separated out and called mind. So Edelman in his writing speaks about 'how the mind works'.

(p. 21). My discussions with Dr Roger Booth helped me to come up with the distinctions I make in this paragraph.

6   See Edelman, Gerald (1992), *Bright Air, Brilliant Fire – On the Matter of the Mind.*

Having a Cup of Tea

To give an example to illustrate these descriptions of brain and mind, let us take the thought of having a cup of tea. Such a thought might be generated by a sense of thirst, but it may also just arise as 'a good idea to give me a break'. The 'information' would be circulated around the neurons through the dendrites. Evaluation would take place that this was a pleasing thing to do, or that there was not enough time to fit in this activity into the planned programme. If the evaluation was positive then the 'information' would be passed to the neurons that would stimulate the muscles to provide the movement necessary to make and drink a cup of tea. What is involved in this process?

- Consciousness of self as a person who can decide about having a cup of tea
- Experience of the pleasure of having a cup of tea
- Experience of making or causing to have made a cup of tea
- Reflection on the balance of need for a cup of tea
- Imagination of the changes in my senses of enjoying a cup of tea, which can lead these senses to anticipate the delight of the result
- Knowledge that imagination is not the reality
- Evaluation of all the possibilities
- Decision.

Creating Pathways

In this example the brain cells would make easy connections with the other neurons because the pattern of transmission would already be well established. You would have made a cup of tea many times before. Because of this a 'pathway', which we might also call in this case a super-highway[7] because it had been travelled so frequently, had already been created to allow the rapid transmission of the 'information' to proceed. However, if the 'information' was new, it would take more effort to evaluate it, and act on it. A correct pathway would have to be created to test the appropriate response, and to work out the best reaction. This would use up more energy in the brain, and there may be a need for some trial and error to take place before the best response could be found. Our first attempts at walking or playing the piano are thus exhausting, but each time we repeat the action successfully the easier it is to achieve the best result next time. This is not only a matter of muscle control, but also brain output. Some experts have likened this process to clearing a pathway through a thick forest. The first time it is hard to find and clear the best path, but once the pathway has been cleared through, it becomes easier to use that path every time we want to pass over it.

---

[7] See Buzan (1993), p. 29.

Retaining 'Information'

The brain has the ability to record 'information' in such a way that the memory track can be used time and time again. The more we use the track the sharper the memory becomes. Thus the brain builds up patterns of appropriate responses to a whole variety of thoughts and stimuli.[8]

The Cosmic Dance

The brain can transmit 'information' as a result of external stimuli, or creative thought patterns, or from the recall of a memory. Such memory can be triggered by a thought, or by an associated stimulus. In our brains one thing connects with others, and this is the miracle of human intelligence. Sir Charles Sherrington, one of the original researchers into the working of the brain who received his Nobel Prize in 1932, used this wonderfully poetic statement about the behaviour of the brain: 'It is as if the Milky Way entered upon some cosmic dance.'[9] Sherrington was trying to describe both the vastness of the activity of which the brain is capable, as well as the intricacy of the linkages between the neurons. The brain is capable of such a multitude of patterns that its outcomes range towards infinity. One neuron links us with the next to make up a sequence like a dance which is on a cosmic scale.

In 1973 Professor Anokhin of Moscow University, at the end of sixty years of investigations, concluded that 'We can show that each of the ten billion neurons in the human brain has a possibility of connections of one with twenty-eight noughts after it.'[10] This only reinforces the concept of the enormous scale of the brain's activity.

The key then to brain function is to use the maximum amount of linkage, or in poetic language, involve as many cells as possible in the 'cosmic dance'. This will provide the maximum number of options and the best mechanism for choices to be made. As we allow the brain to work to the maximum we can explore new ways of doing things, and also determine the consequences for oneself and for others of the proposed course of action. The faster the computer-like brain can function the easier it is for the mind to exercise its thinking and choosing function.

Working to a Set Pattern

At first glance it would seem best for the mind to follow a few well-worn patterns of processing 'information', evaluation and response. In that way life would be kept simple and behaviour straightforward within a safe and limited band. When energy levels are low that is clearly the best option to take. This may explain why human beings when under pressure fall back on a well-tried course of action. In

---

[8] Buzan (1993), p. 35 comments: 'Our brains tend to look for patterns and completion.'
[9] Quoted by Buzan (1993), p. 27.
[10] Quoted by Buzan (1993), p. 29.

these circumstances the cultural norms come to the forefront. In times of famine, war and loss, the routine is set out clearly and rigidly followed.

In times of fear the brain on behalf of the mind is busy processing possible responses. It becomes very focused on the task in hand. The 'dance' is concentrated on finding responses to the causes of the fear. Previous experience is summoned to assist and the dance may become circular as attempts are vigorously made to find an escape route out of the fear. The brain seems to become easily 'tired', and little interest is shown in a wider range of possibilities. Only when the brain works out a suitable response to the fear does the mind relax and look for wider issues to consider. So we arrive at a process of coping with the fear, or of dismissing it as no longer relevant or indeed real.

Creative Energy

However, when the situation allows for more energy to be available the mind, using the brain, is able to explore a greater variety of options. New pathways are discovered and new thoughts and plans are appropriate.[11] These are times of enlightenment and creative thinking, both for the individual and for society.

Two Sides of the Brain

Research has also tried to discover whether different parts of the brain were responsible for processing different activity. In the late 1960s, another Nobel Prize winner Professor Sperry of California, shared his research into the outer shell of the brain which is known as the cerebral cortex.[12] He believed that this was divided into two halves or hemispheres, each of which was responsible for some dominant functions. He postulated that the right hemisphere was concerned with the intellectual functions of rhythm, spatial awareness, the big picture, imagination, daydreaming, colour and dimension. He believed that the left hemisphere was concerned with data, words, logic, numbers, sequence, linearity, analysis and lists. Subsequent research[13] has shown that this view is a little too limited. It seems true that each hemisphere can most easily process the listed types of information. It is also true that both parts are capable of dealing with these functions, but that each part specializes in their particular areas. We know that damage to a certain part of the brain can cause loss of function, but it seems that the other neurons in the brain can also take up the required actions and slowly a new pathway through the forest is created. This may never be as easy to operate, but it can fulfill the requirements to some extent.

---

[11] See Calvin (1997), pp. 18–19.
[12] See Buzan (1995), pp. 17–18 for a fuller description of Professor Sperry's research.
[13] Buzan (1995), p. 18 tells how Professor Zaidel at the University of California 'discovered each hemisphere contains more of the "other side's" abilities than had been previously thought, and that each hemisphere also is capable of a much wider and more subtle range of mental activities.'

Discarding 'Information'

We are well aware that the brain does not retain most of the information it receives or generates. If this were not the case we would be constantly in a state of overload and brain exhaustion. For example, our eyes give us a picture of the whole room when we are introduced to a person for the first time, but the brain usually retains only a few details about that person. Our memory of that person may simply be associated with gender, something about their face and clothing, and anything unusual – such as the person wore glasses, or sat in a favourite chair. The rest of the picture, including the details of the room, are probably not retained. The mind has diminished the neuron signals in the brain on the grounds that the details in the room are not 'valuable' or important. The brain therefore seems to be naturally organized to discard, or as we might now say, not establish a pattern concerning, most of the detail that it receives. There is obviously a major screening process taking place to eliminate the unnecessary. What the brain does remember are those things that have a major impact on us, or make an association for us with an established pattern; those things that arouse our emotions; and those things which we repeat in frequent thought patterns within the first hour and again in the next hour after receiving the information. In this repetition it is an advantage if the thought is turned into an action, for example, through speech or writing.[14] We can say that it is what we tell ourselves again and again that we remember. These are issues which I want to examine in more detail in the next chapter which I have entitled 'Discovering How Memory Works'.

The Search for Progression and Completion

Our brains have another attribute which needs to be highlighted at this point. The 'dance' likes to have both a pattern and a completion. The brain welcomes thoughts that have a progression and an ending. It is set up to search for these. It is said that our brain cells work in systems of one hundred. Maybe that is why we find that it is well within our capability to count to one hundred! To perform this mental feat seems satisfying. The exercise has progression as we reach each sub-group of ten. It then has a sense of relief and conclusion when we come to the number 100. Take another few examples. When we have received some information on a topic we look for more until we achieve a complete picture. If we smell bread baking in the oven, we are drawn to see whether it is cooked, and when it is we want to taste it, and pass comment on its goodness. When we listen to scraps of information about an incident our brains work to find a pattern to the account and to search for a suitable outcome or ending. That is why our brain is so excited about scraps of gossip. It searches for the full story as our 'curiosity' is aroused. The brain searches for the whole picture, and teases us with excitement until it has enough of the story to be satisfied. If it does not receive a full picture, it is likely to make it up – true or not!

---

[14] See Buzan (1993), p. 36.

Finding Patterns

When we receive new 'information' our mind function tests it against the patterns already held in the memory. If it fits, we feel satisfied. If it jars, our minds probe to find out why.[15] The result may be that our brain rearranges the pattern to incorporate the new 'information', or that our mind rejects the new 'information' as impossible, and seeks to dismiss it or amend it.

The 'Information' Process

When I have used the word information in this chapter with a single quotation mark before and after the word, I am using 'information' in a special sense. It refers to anything transmitted around the process of the brain. This 'information' is sent as an electrico-chemical charge from one neuron to another down the dendrites across the end spikes or buttons. These movements form the linkage that create the pattern of thoughts and responses. As we have seen, it is a simultaneous process with traffic flowing in and out.

The 'information' can be broken down into five major categories:[16]

- What is *received* from the sense organs
- What is *held* in the memory
- What is *analyzed* against the patterns already established
- What is *sent out* in the form of instruction for movement of body, including speech, written communication, and other muscular action
- What is *restricted* in the form of control over actions or thoughts – these are the 'shalt not' messages of the brain.

It is important to notice that all such 'information' is moving in an integrated and simultaneous process. As we are receiving 'information', we are sending out 'information' to respond to it. As we are responding and receiving we are storing some of it. As we are receiving, responding and storing 'information' so our minds are analyzing it and seeing where it fits or does not fit already established patterns. As our mind is doing all that, it is also being creative in formulating new responses, including the possibility of new thoughts and new actions. And all the time our mind is calling on its control mechanisms to see if it considers it to be right to be thinking about the matter or instructing the brain to cause the nervous and muscular systems to act in a certain way.

In 1997 Professor Steven Pinker explained his computational theory of the working of the mind and related it to neuroscience. This how he describes the physical functions of the brain as it processes 'information':

> The axon (the long output fiber) of a neuron is designed, down to the molecule, to propagate information with high fidelity across long separations, and when its electrical

---

[15] Calvin (1997), p. 14 comments: 'Substantial incoherence is unpleasant.'
[16] See Buzan (1993), p. 36.

signal is transduced to a chemical one at the synapse (the junction between the neurons), the physical format of the information changes while the information remains the same. And as we shall see, the tree of dendrites (input fibers) on each neuron appears to perform the basic logical and statistical operations underlying computation.[17]

The process is indeed mind-stretching, but not beyond our comprehension. As you have been reading what I have written, so your brain has been sorting out its responses, and trying to find patterns of association with what is familiar to your thinking. Your brain then links these patterns with the new information and retains these linkages. It seeks to find a sense of wholeness in the new material and will repeat the dance until it makes at least temporary sense. The mind may ask the brain for more information to complete the story and may raise a number of questions which it hopes will be answered. It may also gather up linked ideas already known until it can formulate its own satisfactory conclusion. The dance in the brain dies down when a feeling of satisfaction is reached, or when another dance absorbs its energy.

An Example of the Process

Let us see whether your brain has arrived at a point of satisfaction in your inquiry into the way it functions by testing the process against an example. As we are applying the discovery into the way the brain and the mind work to our involvement in liturgy, I will use an experience connected with worship for the example.

You walk into a church to attend a service. Your eye scans the seats and sends a picture of available options as information to the brain. The brain sorts out the information against previously used patterns. In the past, nine times out of ten you have chosen to sit in the sixth row from the front of the church, on the left-hand side. The information from the eye links with the established patterns it has stored to tell you that the usual seat is available. However memory informs you that a friend has asked you to sit with them for this service because that friend's son has recently departed overseas to take up a job in another country. That memory thought stops you automatically following the established pattern and sitting in your familiar seat.

The mind instructs the brain to send information to the eye to scan the church again to see whether your friend is already seated, and if so where that seat is located. The brain also sends a message to your muscles to make you stop walking towards your usual seat until more information is available. The eye responds to the request for information and locates the likely image of your friend, seated in a pew on the right-hand side of the church. It sends this image to the brain which relays it around until it is able to match the new image against the recorded memory of your friend. The new image matches the general outline of your friend, and the usual pattern of hair and head shape. The mind concludes that it is indeed your friend, without the need to check the facial details from the front. The mind instructs the brain to send a further request to the eye to check some other details

---

[17] Pinker (1999), p. 83.

such as clothing, to confirm the person is indeed your friend and that there is a spare seat alongside. The eye returns a positive response on both counts, and the brain passes information to the muscles to move in the direction of the noted seat.

At the same time the brain is stimulated by the thought in the mind as to what you should say to your friend when you greet them. Should you say words of easy greeting and warmth, or pose a question about how your friend is feeling now that her son has gone overseas? Such a thought associates itself with other thoughts as to how you would respond in such circumstances to the various possible approaches. A thought of some anxiety arises and passes information to the brain to instruct the heart to beat a little faster to provide more energy to the brain to help it process the various possibilities. The mind settles on a course of action and the brain passes information to the lips and facial muscles. You smile as you move alongside your friend and state the remembered fact: 'You asked me to sit with you today.' The touch of your friend's hand passes on a message to assure the brain that there is nothing to fear and that your friend is pleased to see you.

The ear passes new information to the brain as your friend says: 'It's all right. Take time to say a prayer.' With this stimulus the brain remembers that you always kneel and say a prayer of preparation when you arrive at your seat for worship. It instructs the body to kneel and the thoughts to focus on a familiar prayer to God. The words of the prayer form on your lips with little effort. The brain has held them in the memory and there is a well-worn track to retrieve the words. You have said the prayer regularly since you learnt it as a child. At the end of the familiar words the brain seems to have gained new energy and allows the mind to begin to have new thoughts.

The brain formulates a prayer about the new situation, about the needs of the friend beside you and your own need to say the most helpful words to that person. The mind, having sorted out the options, instructs the brain to turn the thoughts into words and your lips move without voice to offer the prayer to God. You find some of the words are more than you would have imagined you could think up yourself. They seem to come from 'beyond' you, but they are still in your brain. The prayer draws to its conclusion and the brain inserts a concluding, and satisfying, Amen. It seems that a sequence of mind/brain activity is complete, and the brain appears to rest for a millisecond before starting on its next activity.

Go back now a few paragraphs and compare the example with the list of the five ingredients of 'information'. Note where each was operative in the example I have just given. When you have identified all five, take a pause of satisfaction!

Taking Note of What We Have Learnt

The discovery of the ways in which our brain/mind works may be of interest to satisfy our curiosity or we may apply it to some of our key activities. In pastoral situations it may give us a better understanding of our reactions to certain events, and even assist us to change to more appropriate behaviour. For example, when I am verbally threatened, I will understand why I can so easily resort to verbal revenge unless my mind instructs my brain to see what alternatives are available, and test how beneficial these might be. I will realize the value of constant practice in these alternatives, and thus prevent myself from becoming regularly involved in verbal battles so that this becomes the established pattern. In another area our discovery of the workings of the brain will help us in learning situations to identify the best ways to retain information and improve our memory. In this book I want to apply the learning about the way the brain/mind works to the theory and practice of liturgy. I believe that there are major implications both for the leader of worship and for the participants.

Application to Liturgical Worship

The way that liturgy for worship is constructed needs to reflect the patterns established by the brain, using its preferences for linkages, association of ideas, and its search for completion. It needs to note the effects of emotion and the stimulus of the senses. Liturgy should take advantage of the desire in the brain to put together the whole picture, and to work with structure and rhythm to satisfy the brain's preferred patterns. Participation in worship can also be enhanced if we know how our brain/mind works. We can draw both on its patterns and its new possibilities. We can recognize the value in familiarity and in novelty, and the balance between them. Worship is focused on the God who was, and is, and will be. In worship we draw on our experience of God in the past at the same time as we look for a new experience of God in the present. Our worship prepares us for our expectation of God in the future, and for our service of action in God's name. In this chapter we have discovered how our minds can hold together the past, the present and the future, and how our brains can operate simultaneously in receiving and in giving out. We have seen how the mind has the function of establishing what is of value and what is not worthy of attention. In our worth-ship we confirm what has supreme value for us and thus we can strengthen the patterns of choice. Much of what we have learnt about the brain/mind seems to fit so readily to all that is involved in the worship of God. This research confirms as 'natural' both the nature and the possibilities of liturgical worship.

Liturgical worship in particular aims to involve all of our senses, and to establish a pattern with progressive steps and a satisfying conclusion. It seeks to let us appreciate the past and the future as well as the present. Liturgical worship therefore relies heavily on memory, and it is time now to look more closely into the discovery of how memory works as part of the overall functioning of the brain.

Chapter 2

Discovering How Memory Works

The previous chapter looked in brief outline at the way the whole brain works. With this background we can now look more closely at how the memory functions of the brain operate. As research into the brain is constantly enlarging the knowledge we have of its working, what follows is the 'best guess' from the available evidence.

Patterns and Recall

We have seen how the brain likes to work with patterns. It is possible that the brain has a built-in capacity to store patterns in such a way that it is easy to repeat such patterns of response whenever 'information' is received that requires reaction. When the eye sees steps in the path we are walking, the brain calls on the established patterns to send signals to the muscles in the legs to make the required adjustments to be able to climb the steps. Obviously mechanical movement requires a multitude of adjustments, so signals are not just given to the leg muscles but to many different parts of the body. What is important for us to note is that the brain is able to recall already established patterns so that it does not need to work out a new response to the 'information' received, when that 'information' triggers a known pattern. So we can say that the brain *remembers* how to walk up steps.

Wired to Imitate

'Wired to imitate' is a phrase that William Calvin uses to describe the human brain's ability to record the incoming data and imitate it to provide a built-in memory pattern.[1] With this observation in mind we could say that we learn to remember. We receive the 'information' and the brain records it. By trial and error it establishes a pattern of responses that allows us to imitate the action perceived. So we may learn as a tiny baby to smile, because we see those closest in bonding to us smile as a gesture of love. We may of course learn the opposite and record a pattern of aggression. If we are wired to imitate then this will have major implications both for behaviour and for liturgy. When in liturgy we receive 'information' in word and action that we are valued, cared for and loved, and that the appropriate response is thanksgiving, acceptance, and return of value (worth-ship) to God, then we are establishing a memory pattern for helpful behaviour. We

---

[1] Calvin (1997), p. 33.

will examine this point further in Chapter 4, but this is a place to note the key connections between our discovery about memory and its implications for our worship.

If it is true that we are wired to imitate, then we can see that the brain is by nature tuned into establishing memory patterns. The brain stores these inputs and the corresponding options for responses, and uses this ability to provide further options (thoughts) which the mind can evaluate in reaching decisions about what to do.

Memory Links

As we saw in the first chapter the brain is capable of working on a vast scale simultaneously. The brain has the ability to draw not just on one pattern but on a whole variety of patterns at the same time. It does this by linkage and association. One pattern links in with another and fires that into action.

To continue with our example of walking up a path. As we walk up the steps the brain may also remember previous occasions when we have climbed up steps. It remembers not only 'how' but 'when'. So the brain may recreate a pattern which remembers when we climbed up the steps to our grandparents' house. This may trigger memories of how we were greeted with affection by our grandparents. The memory of the steps to their house evokes a memory of the feelings we had in our relationship with them. Such feelings may be linked with the current feelings of sadness because they are dead. The memory of past events creates in the brain current feelings which may affect our bodies. We may shed a tear or find a lump in our throat as we climb the steps on this pathway in front of us. In the brain we are remembering our grandparents as though they were present. We can feel again their warmth of affection, and at that very same moment feel again the sadness of their loss. We may even 'hear' again their words of encouragement or guidance. We may still want to follow their advice as if they were present, hearing their words: 'Always tell the truth'; 'Look smart, and clean your shoes in the morning'; 'Now make it up with your sister/brother.' Through memory the past becomes present and affects our future behaviour.

The linkage of memory patterns has a powerful effect on our interpretation of present events. When we hear a noise in the night the brain searches for all the remembered linkages. We note that that sort of noise is linked to a cat jumping down from the roof, or to the wind blowing over a watering can, or to a child falling out of bed, or to an earthquake rocking a building. If the brain is satisfied that the noise is identified with a memory of a similar noise which required no responsive action, then the brain will signal to the body to relax. If the mind considers action is required because it has deleted the other options, then the brain will move to recall and repeat the appropriate response. If the 'information' cannot be matched with stored patterns, the mind may choose to order an investigation. Such action may be accompanied by urgent messages of remembered caution that the noise might have been caused by a violent burglar. Such an illustration makes it sufficiently clear for us to note the way linkages occur to determine our current feelings and future actions.

Building Up Memory

We have seen how the brain stores up patterns of response and patterns of feelings as well as facts. Yet you and I know that it is hard to remember much of the 'information' that our brains receive. When we are young we seem to think that our elders expect us to remember everything. 'I've forgotten' seems to be no excuse for a failure to remember things that are required to be done. Adults of course know that they can only remember with a great deal of effort, and so they devise ways of helping the brain in its memory tasks. We make up shopping lists and write down things to be done today. We take pictures to record our holidays so that we can remember and recall their pleasure (and of course the painful and funny stories we tell are another way we do this). As adolescents and then young adults we learn the tricks of study retention. We make notes, use highlighter pens in different colours, create sequences of letters as the key to remember paragraph headings for examination answers, and repeat the vital points to ourselves at frequent intervals until they are embedded in the memory.

So how do our brains remember?

'Repetition in itself increases the probability of repetition.'   So says Tony Buzan.[2] In the first chapter we saw that repetition creates a superhighway in the brain and how the brain stores the remembered details. So it is true to say that we remember best what we recall frequently from the stored information. We can remember our telephone number if we use it day after day or record it frequently in writing. Once we begin to use it infrequently because we do not need to ring home or have no reason to write it down, then it becomes increasingly difficult to remember our own number. We all have this experience.

I assume that the reason children were taught their mathematical tables was that by daily repetition and then usage they would have them permanently stored in the memory. Once children did not need remembered tables to carry out calculations, for that became the work of a calculator, all a child needed to remember was how to insert numbers on the key pad and press the multiplying (or other) function key. Many of the children who have learnt their tables find they no longer remember them because they have no reason to use the memory. So where there is no repetition, there is no memory. If this experience is correct then we can say that we do not remember the original memory, but the latest repeated memory. When we apply this to liturgy, we observe that we do not remember the first occasion of memorizing the Lord's Prayer, but the last time we repeated the Lord's Prayer.

We retain items from the start of the information flow.   When the information is fresh, when it begins a sequence, then that is the information that is more easily retained. So the opening words of a book, the first scene in a film, the first few seconds of a service of worship or a sermon, these are the items that create a brain pattern which has the possibility of being retained. After this it is as if the brain

---

[2]   Buzan (1993), p. 29.

gets tired and struggles to absorb the information. Such retention is known as the *primary effect*.

I expect that this is the reason for the use of headlines in a newspaper, and for the short summary of the main items given at the start of a newscast, and for the place of vital importance that speech writers give to their opening lines which aim to capture the attention of the audience. When the old game of 'remember objects on a tray' was played it was always easier to recall the first three items than those that came in the middle of the sequence. The primary effect was at work, and many were successful to this point, but only those who used other remembering skills won the game.

We retain items from the conclusion of a sequence.   The memory seems also to retain items that are at the end of a learning occasion. What we last read, or heard, or observed, can be retained in our memories. This has been called the *recency effect*. The last pattern created does not seem to be overlaid with another item of information immediately, and so the brain has time to repeat it to itself so that it starts to be retained. We seem to be able to remember the conclusion of a good speech, the last episode of a film, the final paragraphs of a book, and the last words of a dying person.

In the act of memory we often repeat the final sequence in our minds just after we have received the information and this helps to reinforce the recency effect. If the final action is connected to the first information, or if the final act impinges on our senses and our emotions, or if it contains a compact summary of the whole so that the completion attribute of the brain is satisfied, then the final items will create an even stronger pattern in the memory.

The recency and concluding effects have important implications for the practice of liturgy. If the worship just fades out it will miss the opportunity to provide a pattern for future memory. The sense of non-fulfillment and dissatisfaction in worship will remain in the mind even when the middle of the sequence of worship was appreciated by the worshipper. When the worship concludes on a strong note, connected to the whole purpose of the worship, the congregation will depart retaining much of the information and the associated feelings in the memory for recall on future occasions.

We retain information associated with existing patterns already established in the brain.   It is easier to remember information which is linked to other aspects of what we are trying to learn. The brain seems to have a desire to build up existing patterns rather than increase the number of pattern files. Add-ons are better than a whole series of new beginnings. Information which is randomly presented is difficult to remember. However, when information is linked together and has an easily followed sequence, the brain is able to absorb a greater number of items.

Let us use the way the eye records an observation as an example. The eye likes to sweep slowly over the beauty of a scene of hills and lakes. It does not like darting backwards and forwards from side to side trying to relate one aspect of the vision to another out of sequence. The signals the eye sends to the brain are best retained when the pictures are sent in smooth succession, so all parts fit together to make a memorable whole. Once the whole picture is established we may want to focus the eye on a small part, but again this picture is best retained if it fits into the larger vision.

In the same way our brain will have difficulty sorting out the meaning of words on a page if these are randomly scattered without shape or sequence. The brain establishes a pattern of expectation about the text which helps it organize and recognize the words and their interrelationship and meaning. The shape of the phrase or sentence will speed up the retention of the words in the memory. One reason why people are able to remember the words of the recent translations of the Lord's Prayer is that the text on the written page has been set out in phrase lines, and these are brief enough to be retained in the visual as well as the mental memory. In turn these correspond to the audio memory and so we are able to hear, see and think the Lord's Prayer as we repeat it from memory.

This observation helps us to understand why we can remember information which is shared with us in a logical sequence. Recorded figuratively it might look like this, where each letter represents a piece of information:

$$A > A+B > A+B+C > D$$

A and D are more easily remembered as they follow the primary and recency effects. B and C are remembered because they are linked to the initial A, and lead to the concluding D.

In liturgy many good Collects will follow such a pattern. A is the address to God which is followed through with its application to B. This is further connected to a situation in C, and this leads to the petition in the conclusion D. A Collect prayer without this linkage and sequence will be difficult to 'receive' in the mind of the congregation, and be even more difficult to remember moments after the Amen has been said at the end. Unless the brain is able to re-pray the main items at that point, the Collect will probably not be able to be recorded in the mind at all, but literally pass over our heads.

We retain information given special emphasis as being outstanding or unique.   In written form these items of information would be heavily underlined, recorded in bold type, or highlighted in a strong colour. In one way or another the brain receives a signal that this item should be placed in a frame marked 'very important'. Such signals are sent both in words and in gestures by parents to children when informing them about the dangers of putting their hands on a hot stove or into the fire. The warning is also emphasized by the repetition of the warning phrase in a short span of time. The child will take note of the information as important. It will be remembered for future as well as present occasions, though it may still not register fully until the child has received the sensation (hopefully slight) of burning from the heat. We will look at this connection between memory and sensation more fully in the next sub-section.

For information to be framed as important and the memory activated, some conditions should be noted. For something to be framed as 'unique' it cannot be crowded with other items given the same category. There is a strict limit to the number of unique items which we can retain in the memory. We can understand this point from the example of the use of the highlighter pen. If most lines on a page are highlighted, then the effect is negated. We cannot retain more than a few lines – and it is better if these lines are not one after another in the text. In the space of a page there is usually only one point that is unique. If there is more than one we will have to read the page very deliberately, or go back over the page to repeat the items with emphasis. So in the time span of a few minutes we can probably only receive *one* piece of unique information. Any overload of unique items will cause the displacement of most others by the one item which for other reasons is memorable.

Those who conduct liturgy are aware of the need for 'framing' and that there can only be a small number of highlights in a service lasting about one hour. For an example of good liturgy take the framing of the passage of Scripture read as the Gospel. It is given a frame by the change in the body position of the congregation – they are asked to stand. This may be further enhanced by the procession of the reader to the centre of the people. The frame is extended in sound by a said or sung response to the announcement of the reading. On the conclusion of the reading there may be silence as a time for recall of the key words, and this is followed by another affirmation. All this movement and wording sends out signals about the importance of the words of Christ and the need to pay attention. The tone of the reader's voice demands attention because of its clarity and urgency. In liturgy this is a unique moment in the service. If there were more than two or three such moments in a service the congregation would become exhausted and confused, and only remember such feelings.

We retain items of information which engage significantly one or more of our senses and evoke strong feelings. We will remember the bonfire and the fireworks at a family gathering because our eyes saw the flames and the sparkles, and our bodies felt the warmth of the fire, and our mouths tasted the potatoes cooked in the embers, and our hearts experienced feelings of fellowship and kinship. The more senses that are employed, the deeper that the remembrance patterns are laid. Future bonfires will call forth the cry of 'You remember' as the brain recalls past experiences and the feelings of human as well as physical warmth.

Those who conduct worship during a retreat will tell you how much people remember when they have engaged many of the senses during the worship. When the cross is touched at times of prayer for those in pain and suffering, such prayer takes on a new dimension and the memory lingers for many years. It is reawakened during future prayers for those in pain even when there is no cross to touch. When candle-light is added, and the smell of incense rises, and a repeated sung refrain concentrates the mind, the occasion will remain firmly fixed in the mind of the worshipper.

The physical nature of the Sacraments of Baptism and Eucharist are no accidents. To proclaim the remembrance that God has for us, and our remembrance of the actions and activity of God on our behalf, the Sacraments will have their 'proper' physical form so that they engage more of our senses than merely hearing. Likewise the laying on of hands in blessing, healing and empowerment are a vital part of our remembrance of such key occasions. The words interpret the actions and the gestures reinforce the tone of importance, yet it is the physical impact on our other senses that often lingers longest in the memory.

We retain those items of information which are of particular interest and significance to us personally. If the information connects with other thoughts already circulating in our brain so that we can make good linkages, so that we are tuned in, then we will find it easier to remember this new information. It may be information which satisfies one of our existing questions, or be very relevant to our current context, or be a description of a scene or situation we have already experienced. The important point to note is that the relevance of the information to the hearer is vital to its retention in that person's memory. The brain keeps seeking for connections and will otherwise quickly disregard information which has no relevance for it.

If you tell me about marble baths suitable for installation in high-rise luxury apartments and I live in a corrugated iron hut on the edge of a shanty town, I may be interested because of the novelty of the information but I will probably not retain the memory because that information is not applicable to my situation.

In liturgy the key places for the test of application are in the sermon and the prayers. The information in the sermon may be of interest to the preacher but if it does not connect with the questions, needs and context of the congregation, it is but a sounding gong. If preachers are unaware of the questions and cries of the congregation through their pastoral visiting, then it is unlikely that they will be in a position to preach a memorable sermon.

Often the prayers of intercession are even less memorable – unless it is for the wrong reason! I have heard leaders of the intercession introduce topics which are of no concern and outside the knowledge of the rest of the members of the group. The group may need to gain that knowledge or grow in their concerns, but such bridges must be built by other means and in other settings. The prayers are like incense, they should arise from the cries of joy, pain and concern already there among the people. They cannot be imposed by the leader.

One of the reasons why 'special' services are so memorable is that they provide the opportunity for a concern of mutual interest to bind the congregation together. If the service responds to such a concern, and each part is linked to the common theme, then the congregation will not only feel satisfaction and fulfillment, but also retain the memory of the service as positive in the building up of their worship skills.

Longer-term Retention of Memories

The above paragraphs explain in outline how the brain inserts information into the short-term memory. Now it is time to try to discover how we retain those memories over a longer span.

The important factor is constant recall. Repetition keeps open the superhighway. It is said that we lose 80 per cent of the details of any information recorded within a period of 24 hours, and that this cannot be recalled; it can only be revisited. What small amount we do retain can be accounted for as follows:

1   We can retain information by doing a summary review within ten minutes of first storing the information. We therefore need space for regular reflection to retain some of what we have put into the short-term memory.

2   Within 24 hours we need to repeat the memory of the information. It is particularly helpful at this point if we can express in speech, writing or graphics *our memory* of the information we have received. To write a diary, to tell a friend on the telephone, to express our feelings will all aid the retention of what we have remembered for 24 hours.

3   Within one week our brain will have completed another sorting process. If we can recall our experience, apply the learning, express its impact on us, then it is likely that we can retain the memory. When considering worship we can see how the pattern of daily and weekly worship fits well within this framework for the retention of memory.

4   Within one month we need to have made choices of options for action if we are to retain the memory on a longer-term basis. The memory will remain longer if we have turned the information into some action. The activity may be of the body or of the mind. This may explain why groups do not work well if they do not carry out an activity within the span of one month. Those groups that meet once a month will only have a strong continuing life if the corporate memory is reawakened by the recall of relationships and memories within that time frame.

Such groups also illustrate that the factors behind short-term memory are important to longer-term memory. When some members of the group ask what the programme was last month, the truth is that they may have been present but the programme made no impact on their thinking, feeling or behaviour. For them there was nothing unique, and the beginning and end were so routine that they were passed over entirely. Others in the same group may have vivid memories of the programme because it had connected with their personal agenda, and they had recalled the information and applied it many times during the month. Again members will recall the names of those other members who related well to them or who had made an impact on them. Those who miss the monthly meetings are hardly likely to know the names of the other members unless they meet them within the month at another gathering. The corporate fellowship has no chance of surviving more than a monthly gap, however much the use of name tags is encouraged. We may well address the name but not meet the person in such circumstances.

Condensing the Memory

William Calvin observes that 'One of the first lessons about working memory is that there's seemingly a limited scratch pad, better suited to a half-dozen items than twice that number.'[3] This is an important factor for all those who must depend on an accurate recall of memory. Using the other factor of association, such people try to condense the information into groups of 'objects'. They have learnt to trigger a wider memory recall from a few short notes, symbols, letters or numbers. Every household shopper knows that you can reduce the shopping list to a few headings.

---

[3]   Calvin (1997), p. 93.

'Eggs' will be the shorthand for a dozen brown eggs of medium size, checked to see that none are cracked. Another example common to us all is the way that many public speakers reduce their notes for a so-called impromptu speech to a few bold headings on a card. Similarly some preachers with well-trained memories can use a few headings to deliver a full sermon. Calvin in the same book has also noted the habit of arranging series of numbers and information into sub-groups, which he calls 'chunking'.[4] An eleven-digit telephone number including the country and the area codes can be recalled more easily if it is arranged in sub-groups such as: 00-33-24-57-54-77-5. That seems more accessible to the brain than the sequence: 3324-5754775.

It is also possible to apply this factor of chunking to the memory of Biblical verses. We can remember a whole series of verses when they are arranged around a key word. Take love as an example. We can recall: 'For God so loved the world that he gave his only Son, so that everyone who believes in him may not perish, but may have eternal life.'[5] Followed by: 'No one has greater love than this, to lay down one's life for one's friends.'[6] Linked up with 'This is my commandment, that you love one another as I have loved you.'[7] Love is the chunk word that triggers the memory of the rest of the words.

The memory also condenses the information by focusing on what the mind has considered to be the key points. When I try and remember last Saturday, the mind will recall something unique, or something that contains much emotion, or something that responded to my context. I may recall last Saturday because it was the day that it rained after a long drought, or because it was my wedding anniversary, or because the doctor came to visit me in my sickness. Everything else about last Saturday may be a great blur. After a week I will remember some selected items but most routine events will have been discarded from my memory. I will not remember what time I woke up or know how long it took to boil the kettle for the first cup of tea, or even what music was played on the radio.

If a service of worship is to be memorable then the memory will condense that experience down to a few brief points. We may remember that we found the prayers helpful though we cannot remember the contents or the wording of any individual prayer. We may remember the theme or short text of the sermon which spoke to our situation. We may more easily remember a special symbol used in the service – the water that splashed on the floor at the baptism or the symbol of the empty tomb at Easter, or the apple we shared at the end of the Harvest Festival. That is the way we remember we were at worship. Our minds have chunked the memory of it into one or two special features of the service.

Such condensing also explains why the memory of the same event often varies for two (or more) different people. Our minds condense the memory to retain only what is of importance for us. Bower and Morrow made this observation: 'Readers tend to remember the mental model they constructed from a text rather than the

---

4   Calvin (1997), p. 92.
5   John 3:16.
6   John 15:13.
7   John 15:12.

text itself.'[8] This does not mean that the event itself did not happen, or necessarily that the memory of one person was deficient. To a large extent the impact of the event is more important for us than the event itself. If no one remembers the event, then the event loses all its significance, and is soon forgotten. The remembrance of the significance given to the event gives the event itself a place in history. This observation has implications in liturgy for both the Eucharist and Baptism. It may also be a key observation for Biblical interpretation where the *remembrance* of the Christ event may be of greater importance than the event itself.

Memory and Language

Those memories that we cannot put into language are in the end difficult to retain. It would seem that when the brain can establish a pattern of words as an outline of the memory then that pattern track can be accessed more readily. As memory is laid down through patterns, it seems appropriate that the pattern of language reinforces the pattern of memory. It is for this reason that when we speak to others about an event and its significance for us, or write it down in a journal within the time sequences we have noted as essential, we can retain much of the detail of the memory. The repetition of a memory when committed to language will establish the pattern of memory on a long-term basis.

In liturgy the repetition of the same words in speech and print has the effect of establishing and then recalling the pattern and significance of the event. Prayer can indeed be offered without words, but the memory of prayer and its significance will be greatly enhanced by the language of the prayer itself. It is also true that the use of symbols with words leads to a very strong pattern of memories.

William Calvin points to the formation of brain patterns, maybe even vibrations, which if printed would look like bar codes.[9] These are the mechanisms which give us an understanding of how the brain might have something similar to a bar code to retain the memory pattern. The brain would recognize the code and respond accordingly. The language of a sentence in liturgy has similarities to a bar code because its words act as a trigger for the memory of meaning and significance. In the brain the 'bar code' may be enhanced by the rhythm of the words or of a musical tune. Likewise in liturgy the rhythm of words and music reinforce the memory triggers. There all these factors work in harmony to produce the desired goal – remembrance of God and of God's memory of us.

Memory and Inspiration

Memory not only recalls the past and repeats its significance and influence on our present state. It also allows creativity and planning for the future. Memory provides

---

[8] Gordon H. Bower and Daniel G. Morrow (1990), 'Mental Models in narrative comprehension', *Science* 247:44–8.

[9] Calvin (1997), Ch. 4.

the material for our mind to arrange new patterns to create the possibilities for future action. Our new thoughts would seem in reality to be a new combination of old thoughts. Out of the basic building blocks we constantly look for new patterns which in turn become the building blocks for the enlarged possibilities. We imitate to learn and then learn to imitate. Many educators have advised those who wanted to have good communication skills in teaching to move step by step from the known to the unknown. The brain by association, linkage, picture completion and sequence is able to rearrange the known to move to a new combination of ideas, which seem beyond our comprehension until the 'penny drops' or the memories drop into a new pattern. Learning is impossible on those occasions when a bridge cannot be created between the known and the unknown. In that case the brain may say to us: 'I have no pattern for that, and I cannot recognize any patterns which I can copy and then reorganize to form a new pattern for future action.'

In theological terms this understanding of brain function is vital. Theology is the science of formulating language (and therefore understanding) about God and God's actions. As God is a mystery 'beyond comprehension', it could be said that doing theology is an impossible task. However what theology does is to build a bridge between the known and the unknown by using the language of metaphor. We borrow the known language to be inspired to discover language for the unknown. Our research shows that this procedure is natural to the brain. It is just how the brain itself works. Out of familiar patterns, recalled from memory, we create new patterns to apply to a different situation. In liturgy this theological language often changes from the third person (language about God) to the second person (the language of relationship). We not only talk about God; in liturgy we address that God, and look for an address in reply. The language we borrow for these addresses is the language of human relationship. We discover that we can know God in action like a loving parent when we address God as 'our Father'. We discover an appropriate response as we join our will with God's will, praying 'your will be done'. In using this language we are not making God a substitute for a human parent. Rather we are using the building block of human relationships to formulate language to know something about our relationship with God. The language of prayer aims to retain and reinforce the memory of this relationship, and to move us on to seek to discover more of the God who, though unknowable, seeks to reveal God's nature to us through the metaphors of human relationships.

We can use the 'notes' of music as an example of the way the brain/mind seems to rearrange the basic pattern to formulate new possibilities. In music there is a given range of set notes. In themselves these notes are of little significance. However when the notes are combined in a sequence, a pattern is established. This is both memorable and something that can also be rearranged to produce a new tune. This tune can in turn be subject to a variety of variations which are the building blocks of a final outcome of a piece of music. There are seemingly endless possibilities for the creation of music, but in essence each one will be a rearrangement of the set patterns. There is only one set of notes, but there are tunes without number.

The way we use language is another example. The basic words can be arranged and rearranged to produce new sentences with new shades of meaning and significance. We even make up the words by copying and combining the basic vocabulary. We may use the memory of words in other languages or for other situations. The keys of the piano become the key board of the computer – in itself a composite word from the Latin meaning 'to think together'. Likewise in liturgy it is the combination of words, music and silence which produces new revelations and experiences of God, which in turn give us the building blocks for our future worship of God.

Memory and Self-identity

Memory is a vital part of our discovery of a sense of self. We remember not only the incident but our part in the incident or our reaction to it. The memory helps us to sort out the 'me' from the 'them', or the 'it'. I remember the food on the table for my birthday, and at the same time I remember myself looking at the food and being happy and hungry. I remember the people who shared the birthday party with me and my reaction to them. In the memories I establish both the event and the experience – and my own objective/subjective responses to them. As Israel Rosenfield puts it so clearly,'My sense of self derives from a certainty that my experiences refer back to me, the individual who is having them.'[10]

For the establishment of a relationship in liturgy I must have a sense of self and a sense of other. Liturgy helps me see myself as a child of God and helps me to see my need of a relationship with God and with the community which shares the liturgy. The words of the liturgy recall the corporate memory of our address to God and God's address to us in worship. At the same time in liturgy we are very conscious of ourselves as being in relationship with God. The 'I' who addresses God is in turn addressed by God and becomes part of the 'we' who have discovered God and search for new ways to reveal the relationship with God, which is the birthright of all humanity.

As children learn who they are from the way that they are addressed by the parent or the caregiver, so worshippers learn who they are from the address of God to them in the memories of the community gathered as the Church in the past and in the present. The new words of the current address are the memories of the old words given new significance and reality in the new context. The language evokes the memories, and the memory inspires the sense of self and of its relationship with the God of worship.

Memory and Liturgy

The brain seems to have the capacity to copy the patterns which it establishes, and then use the copy both for recognition and for the creation of new combinations of copies or parts of them. Memory is therefore vital for the construction of the future

10 Israel Rosenfield (1992), *The Strange, Familiar, and Forgotten: An Anatomy of Consciousness*, p. 87.

as well as of the past. It is also vital for the establishment of the sense of self and the recognition of other.

Liturgy serves to reconnect us to the past and to shape us for the future. It helps to affirm our relationship with God and with the community. It assists us to see that we have a place in the universe as a person of value and worth.

Without memory there can be no liturgy. Without the language and actions of liturgy our memory of who we are and who we should become would fade. 'The first step in liquidating a people is to erase its memory', said Milan Herbl.[11] Thus the first step in liquidating the people of God is to separate them from a living liturgy. Without a memory there can be no liturgy. Without a liturgy there can be no memory of God for the people. This dire warning is reinforced by the way the brain seems to work. The next chapter applies such learning and warning to our remembrance of God in the liturgy.

---

[11] Quoted in Charles Elliott (1995), *Memory and Salvation*, p. 11.

Chapter 3

Remembering God

Creating Relationships

At the heart of all worship is the act of remembrance. This leads to thanksgiving, praise and the honouring of the object of worship. In Christian worship the object of remembrance is the God who is revealed in Jesus Christ and known through the power of the Holy Spirit. Each occasion of worship allows the worshipper to recall consciously the relationship formed with Christ, and this recollection forms links with all the previously stored experiences that the worshipper has of the presence of the Spirit of Christ in the past.

In terms of our discoveries on the way our brain and mind work, we can see how the thought of God triggers the pathways of connections linking us with memories from the past. These memories flow through long familiar avenues of mental activity to give rise to the warmth found in our relationship with God, and to the glow of gratitude for all the affirmations and gifts that we have received. In the expanding circuit of the brain the worshipper can link in to a variety of experiences and knowledge which in turn enhance the opportunity of worship. This mental activity re-establishes the relationship in a way which not only picks it up from where it left off, but also adds new dimensions from the present experience. For this reason worship is never static – it does not stand still – but is a continuous movement which flows into the future.

We can liken the activity of worship to the flow of a river. Worship has its source at a given point from a collection of tiny contributors which are not easily identified until they come together in a visible stream. From this point of departure, which can always be traced but is never able to be repeated, worship gathers noticeable strength as it picks up new contributions and forms a constant flowing stream which can be easily entered and experienced. This type of worship feeds the life which surrounds it, giving it sustenance and refreshment. Like the waters of a river such worship is both individual and corporate though the lines of definition between the two are always blurred. The individual can own the experience of worship while at the same time recognizing that their life of worship is intermingled with the worship of the community. The experience of the individual is always enlarged by the experience of others at worship, and even further by the corporate worship of the whole body which is more than the sum of its parts.

Recalling the Nature of God's Being

To remember God is to recall the nature of God's being. In diagram form one idea or description about God is, through memory, linked with a circle of associated words or phrases. The linkage processes of the brain allow us to keep together all the various attributes of God to provide the fuller picture. This is the way it might appear:

As Christians we affirm that Christ has put a human face and a human heart to the mystical concept of God. In Jesus Christ the nouns are turned into active verbs so that ideas become visible as divine activity. In worship the noun 'Life-Giver' is linked to the act of resurrection and the promise of life lived to the full, now and in eternity. From our understanding of the way the mind and the memory work we can see the activity of worship as tree-shaped. The central trunk of the concept of God links the branches of the various activities of God so that who God is, is expressed in what God does for us as a community and as individuals within it. To speak of God as 'Affirmer' allows the worshipper to experience the activity of God in listening, forgiving, reshaping, uniting, comforting and strengthening people so that they live life to the full. To touch the hem of Christ's garment in search of forgiveness and value[1] opens the way for all the other experiences of God that are offered through worship. In the works of Christ we see concrete examples of the way God is active in our world. As our brain processes these incidents, so it links them with the experiences we corporately and individually have of similar situ-

---

[1] Matt. 9:21, Mark 5:27, Luke 8:44.

ations that our memory recalls as we worship. These remembrances renew our present relationship with the God whom we affirm as active in giving us the fullness of life and love.

Remembering God, Not Ourselves

On each worship occasion we reaffirm the experience and faith of the community of the Church as to the nature and activity of God. The words of praise, thanksgiving and honour can be traced throughout the whole sequence of corporate worship. One of the delusions of some worship is to set the focus on the assembly and its members, and not on the nature and activity of God. In part this reflects the emphasis on 'me' in modern secular society. This 'me' can be the small group as well as the individual. To focus on this 'me' is to leave unsatisfied the inner longing for the sense of 'other' beyond the limit of my own being and circle. If we focus only on ourselves and not God, worship will not lift us up but dumb us down.

For the same reason the prayers of an individual that only focus on individual need will become empty and unfulfilling. If in prayer I do no more than talk about myself, I might as well talk to myself. True prayer to God begins with our remembrance of God and the nature of the relationship. This results in finding new purpose and assurance in my life as valuable – whatever the circumstances – to the divine will and purpose for all of humanity and for all of creation. God will still be experienced as paying attention to my needs and concerns, but in the context of the purpose of a loving and life-giving God. As the mind works in worship I need to follow the pathway which best links with the desired goals. If I follow the pathway of God the outcomes will be different to those I would attain if I follow the pathway of self. If I follow the pathway of self, the act of prayer will be turned in on itself. The great mystics have encouraged us to follow the pathway of contemplation of God to the point where we are so absorbed into the being of God that the importance of self loses its force and hold over us.[2] This gives new meaning to Christ's exhortation to his disciples to lose life in order to find it.[3] Most worshippers do not reach the point that the mystics call 'unity' with God, but they will experience the delights of seeing the wider vision and the greater purpose of God. Each time in prayer worshippers advance further towards this goal the mental highway will be cleared to make it easier to attain their joyful desire.

---

[2] The modern mystic Henri Nouwen writes: 'When I pray, I enter into the depth of my own heart and find there the heart of God, who speaks to me of love. And I recognize, right there, the place where all of my sisters and brothers are in communion with one another.' (Durback, Robert (ed.) (2002), *Henri Nouwen, In My Own Words*, p. 30).

[3] Matt. 10:39, Mark 8:35, Luke 9:24.

Repetition

The formula for seeing that our worship and prayer is focused on God rather than on ourselves lies in the repetition of the known and the familiar as the link which provides the sequence of establishing God as both the subject and the object of our worship. The instability of modern society finds repetition and familiarity 'boring'. However such an attitude fails to see that foundations must be established on which further activity can rest. In the field of education and sport the failure of novelty and inordinate flexibility is driving a new 'back to basics' campaign. Maybe it is time that we applied the same evidence to the sphere of worship. Our minds are built to move from the familiar into the new situation. Our minds need to find the patterns of familiarity in order to allow the extra energy to be available to tackle the new situations which need attention. Christian worship is designed to allow memory to bring us up to speed so that we can apply the recalled truths about God to our new and critical situations. It is not helpful to begin all things *de novo*. This is because much of life runs to a pattern, and can be dealt with routinely. In addition what is really new needs to be dealt with 'in context' of the known. In the end the givens are more vital to our future than the novelties of the present.

This may explain the long experience of monastic prayer as based on a repetitive cycle, particularly involving the repetition of the Psalms.[4] The familiar phrases in the Psalms linked the experience of God in the past to the current context. Worship became the 'vessel' which held the relationship of the worshipper and God, and which allowed the new refreshment of God's love in context to be tasted and enjoyed. The vessel is essential to the action of drinking, but it is not the source of the sustenance in itself. In worship the Spirit is discovered in the form, but the form is not the Spirit. It takes time for this truth to dawn on the worshipper, but the mind is used to making such connections. It can use the familiar form and symbol to link the brain with the living relationship which is at the heart of worship. Similarly the wedding ring is not the substance of the marriage but it can convey the memory of the relationship and reactivate the love between the spouses. Likewise the form of worship is not the substance of the Divine, but it can convey the memory of the relationship and reactivate the feelings of love, loyalty and value between the worshipper and God, and between God and the worshipper.

Practical Implications for Worship

We need to turn these general comments into answers to the key question: 'How can worship connect us more effectively to God as we use our memory faculty?' I see seven responses to that question.

---

[4] See Brian Wren's comments on the use of the Psalms at Cluny (1200 CE): 'Old brothers have sung the chants so often that they are stored in the memory' (Wren (2000), p. 24).

1. *Worship can provide the links we need to be in touch again with the foundations of our relationship with God.* Through worship our memories will quickly recapture the relationship at the point where we were last conscious of its importance for us. Like a handshake that reunites two friends and expresses all the value and gratitude for the relationship firmly established, so worship unites us speedily in our relationship with God. Those who are new to worship find it more difficult to move into this resumption of the relationship. They wonder at the way the 'old hands' slide so easily into the mode of worship. The old monk can enter the stall and in a few seconds become engrossed in the adoration of God. The reason for this is that the depth of memory is so profound that the presence of God is brought into reality with an ease that amazes the newer worshipper. The same is equally true of the faithful lay worshipper who has spent years 'on their knees before the Lord'. The act of worship renews the relationship and reinvigorates it. The more familiar the place and the form of worship the easier the memory can pick up the past and make it present. For this to occur the form of the worship seems even more vital than the place of worship as those who have been imprisoned for their faith tell us. They have revealed that despite the dislocation they can re-enter the relationship with God through recalling the basic forms of worship committed to their memory, be it the Lord's Prayer, known Psalms or other Scripture verses, or familiar prayers of thanksgiving, confession and praise. The repetition of the basics is an essential part of private and public worship. Current fashion for endless variety does not assist the building up of those links in worship which best allow for the rapid recapture of the feelings of relationship. Within the familiar form there is indeed need for the recognition of the current context, but the familiar form has its primary place in providing the means for the memory to pick up the relationship from the point when it was last experienced.

2. *Worship has the role of providing the connection with the whole of God's character and being.* As we relate to God in a way that is especially appropriate for this moment, it is important that through worship we are in touch with the totality of God's revelation to us. Our view of God can become distorted if we concentrate too much on the immediate context and do not recall all the ways God has been revealed to us through individual and corporate worship in the past. Knowledge of God and God's activity has to be kept in balance or it becomes dangerously distorted. In such ways heresies are born. Our worship provides links for the memory to touch as much as possible of the whole character of God revealed to us. The 'occasional' worshipper is handicapped if the only remembrance of God for them is focused on a narrow range of worship experiences. To attend worship in the context of a funeral, a wedding, and a Christmas pageant can hardly build up a relationship with a God who embraces the whole of creation and the whole of life. In the same way services of worship which are too highly focused on one aspect of God will deprive worshippers of the links with the whole of God's character. A chosen focus set within the whole framework of worship should allow adequate reference to be made both to it and to the other aspects of God's being. This puts the particular focus in the context of the wider picture of God's being and activity. I believe this is why the Great Thanksgiving Prayer at the Eucharist is so broadly based in its gratitude for all God's activity on our behalf.

The sweep of the prayer includes God's activity in creation, redemption, sanctification and eternal life. Attempts to foreshorten the breadth of this prayer should be resisted as it will then not provide the links of memory that allow us to grasp the whole nature of God.

3. *Worship has the purpose of linking us with the whole community of those who worship God.* As a corporate activity worship allows us to enter into the memory of the community which in the past as well as in the present worships the same God. The relationship with God is one in which I, as an individual, participate in a relationship which God's people have had, and still have, with the God who has been revealed over many generations. We come to know God, not only from our own experiences, but also from the corporate experiences of our ancestors in the faith. This community has shared their experiences in person and in writing in such a way that we can deepen our relationship with God. Individuals from their own experiences cannot fathom the possible breadth of the relationship with the Divine, so we are reliant on others to enlarge what we ourselves have received. The community needs to share these experiences through its current members in a particular locality and through the stories of those who have lived in a different age or place. Worship is designed to be the opportunity to create this corporate memory. There we hear what the prayers and praises 'mean' for our fellow worshippers. There we hear the experiences of the saints of the past, and the saints of other parts of the wider community, and allow these experiences to enlarge our relationship with their God and our God. It is for this reason that there is a legitimate place in worship to tell the stories of faith. Such stories spring from Scripture, blossom in the lives of the saints, and show fruit in the life stories of the worshipping community.

4. *Worship inspires us to search for further truth about our relationship with God.* Because the mind searches for completion so in worship we are inspired to enter more fully into the relationship with God which is always expanding. This creates the excitement we find in worship as we look for God to reveal more about the divine nature and character to us. Memory is seen by some to mean the recall of what is already known. Yet our research into the way the mind functions shows us that memory may begin in the past but then triggers a search for the outcomes of what is recalled, and this leads to further discoveries in the present. For example worship can link us to the memory of God's forgiveness in the past in such a way that God's loving forgiveness can apply to our present situation and the acknowledgment of a recent act of wrongdoing. Worship also links us with the memory of God's loving actions in Jesus Christ as they are recorded in the Scriptures proclaimed during worship. The purpose of this proclamation is to provoke us to see how the loving actions of God apply to our context in the present. So worship inspires the constant search for new applications of the relationship and for new truth to be revealed about the God whom we worship and value. Through worship we are drawn step by step into this deeper relationship and the mind creates an eagerness to know more of God until we come 'face to face' in full understanding and love.

5. *Worship assists us to see the present situation in relation to the past and to the future.* Worshippers can often be overwhelmed by the circumstances of the present. By entering into worship we can link up with the support and guidance we have received from God in the past and feel affirmation in the current situation. A familiar hymn or Scripture passage in a funeral service can fulfill this function for us. The words (and the music) will bring back memories of the comfort and strength we have received in the past when faced with the reality and sorrow of the death of a person close to us. That hymn and verse will recall not only the sorrow of loss but also the experience of God's hope and love which was ours in the previous situation. At the same time we are being prepared in the future for the death of ourselves, learning to trust the God who promises resurrection and eternal life as the fuller word on the mortality of being human. Again the stability of the service of worship will assist the participants to make the links with the past and the future. The fragility of life is becoming the dominant theme in world society as uncertainty and instability shatter the easy dream that material progress would make life safer for the majority of humanity. Climate conditions, as well as human evil and carelessness, have increased anxiety over the future, for the individual and for the world as a whole. Those who share in worship know how it builds up trust in a relationship with God who gives us hope in times of despair and courage in the face of adversity. Such a feeling of trust cannot be produced instantly any more than a true friend can be found at a moment's notice in time of need. The context of worship is the place for the long-term development of our relationship with God on which we can draw in times of stress.

6. *Worship provides us with the opportunity to use the stable and the familiar to reflect on how to do the will of God in the current context.* Worship is about obedience as well as adoration. Those who worship God dedicate themselves to the service of God. Worship is about what we do as well as what we say. When faced with the challenge of action our memory, built up through worship, recalls the key instructions from God which will shape our actions. Our memory will be of the words of Jesus Christ, and also of the struggle of the Spirit within us to discern the will of God in a particular circumstance. We will recall the principles on which Christian action is based, even when the current context is different to those other times when we have been confident that we have done the will of God. This aspect of fulfilling the divine will and purpose lies behind the place of intercessory prayer in the programme of worship. Intercessory prayer is part of the work of the Christian community and in it the struggle to discern the will of God is voiced. It is not enough in these prayers to simply pray for a list of people and objects. Our prayers need to express what we want for these people and for ourselves if we are to be partners with Christ in the fulfillment of the prayers we offer. As we express what we want God to do for individuals and groups so we will be guided to see how such wishes can be brought about. Our experience of how God responds to our prayers will be part of the way those for whom we pray build up their relationship with God.

7. *Worship will create new memories of how God has interacted with us, and this will carry us into a deeper relationship with God.* In worship the memories of

the past become refreshed and reinvigorated in such a way that we know that we have been engaged by the grace of God. This can lead us to affirm words used in some recent liturgical writing: 'The Lord is here. God's Spirit is with us.' Without a memory of God we could not recognize the presence of God. Once we have encountered the God we recognize from our previous memories, then we are able to create a new memory of the gracious presence of God on this occasion. We meet God again in a way that is always new, yet does not break with the continuity of memory. Worship may help us broaden and amend some memories of God in the past, but there is always an element of continuity once we have had time to reflect. The fullness of God that Christ revealed was in continuity with the God of the people of Israel, even though it was not defined by the past. Our worship helps to make the link of continuity while at the same time allowing us to lay down new experiences of God. These may amend the picture of God which we had falsely held, or the deficiency of which we were not previously aware. All of us need to be open to the creativity of worship as new memories are added to deepen our relationship with God.

The Passover Experience

These aspects of worship are well illustrated in the passage of Scripture which links the historical exodus of the Hebrew people out of Egypt with the ritual worship of God year by year in the festival of Passover. Within Chapters 12 and 13 of the Book of Exodus are embedded the kernel of faith Israel held in the saving acts of their God, and the way that they are to make memorial of these acts in their annual worship. As one commentator has said:

> The intended goal is that the later Israel feel itself one with the Israel of the exodus and will re-live it as an event they were personally involved in . . . The past is to be kept alive in two ways:
>
> (1) by making it *visible* through religious ritual (Ex. 13:3, 7, 16; cf. Ex. 12:14, 17, 25, 42);
> (2) by making it *audible* through explanation (Ex. 13:8, 9 ['on your lips'], 14f; cf. Ex. 12:26, 27a).
>
> . . . Through the observance of three customs: Passover, Matzoth and dedication of the firstborn, the past is as it were to be transformed into the present.[5]

These observations sum up well the way that memory functions in worship.

Another earlier commentator on the Passover in his extended thesis on the subject has highlighted the use of the Hebrew root *zkr* (remembrance) in three key passages in Exodus:

---

[5] Cornelius Houtman (1996) *Historical Commentary on the Old Testament: Exodus Vol. 2*, pp. 143–4.

- Exodus 12:14 [attributed to P]
  And this day shall be unto you for a memorial [Hebrew *zikkaron*], and you shall keep it a feast to the Lord: throughout your generations ye shall keep it a feast by an ordinance for ever.

- Exodus 13:3–4 [attributed to JE]
  Remember (Hebrew *zkr*) this day, in which ye came out from Egypt, out of the house of bondage; for by strength of hand the Lord brought you out from this place.

- Exodus 13: 9 [attributed to JE]
  And it shall be a sign unto thee upon thine hand and for a memorial (Hebrew *zikkaron*) between thine eyes, that the law of the Lord may be in thy mouth for with a strong hand hath the Lord brought thee out of Egypt.[6]

So the remembrance of the event allows the worshipper in each generation to participate through worship in the experience which led to the relationship between Israel and their God. This relationship was a corporate relationship between the people and their God, and yet it was also the basis of the relationship between each worshipper and the God made known to them. God was a God who acted to save. God was a God who created an intimate relationship. God was a God who commanded obedience. God was a God who by acting in the past had established a relationship for the present and the future.

As the commentators show the Passover festival itself was built around the memory of the festival for the beginning of the New Year and gathered to itself elements of the enthronement of the king or tribal leader. This should not surprise us. The experience of God in one situation allows us to attach new and old experiences to a common worship event. The God who acts to revive the cycle of the agricultural year, will also act to revive the fortunes of those who feel lost in powerlessness and despair. It may be true that

> The original purpose of the paschal meal was to re-cement ties of kinship, infuse new life into the family, and renew the bonds of mutual protection at the beginning of each year.[7]

Yet the act of God in the Exodus created new ties of kinship, infused new life and gave protection to those who would be called the people of God. In the time of Jesus Christ the same actions were taken by God in the 'new' exodus when the death of the first born created a new body of the redeemed and empowered the new people of God. As Houtman states:

> The keeping alive of the memory of the deliverance fixes Israel's mind on the fact that it belongs to YHWH and has obligations towards him. But remembrance of the exodus

---

[6] J.B. Segal (1963), *The Hebrew Passover*, pp. 60 and 65.
[7] Theodor Gaster (1958), *Passover, Its History and Traditions*, p. 18.

creates expectations as well. The certainty that YHWH saved his people in the past offers hope for fresh saving acts of YHWH.[8]

When Christians celebrate Holy Week they would do well to remember the festival of Passover and recall the corporate memory of God's saving acts in a wider context as the early Church would have done. Even the memory of the enthronement of the king at this new year festival has its place in the Easter liturgy. The resurrection of Christ, as made clear in the doctrine of the Ascension, declares God's favour on the Son who is to reign for ever and ever. Through the memory of past worship in many generations, the ever widening circle of meaning becomes clear, and the worshipper gains further insight into the character and actions of God.

Tangible Liturgy

One of the main features in the Passover Festival as laid down in the Exodus passages is the impact of tangible liturgy. The worship is by households in a setting that allows maximum participation. Liturgy here is about action illuminated by words. The worshippers at the feast are commanded to give their full attention to this work of liturgy in priority to any other work. Worship here is not an optional extra. Not to participate in this worship is to cut yourself off from the community. In this worship no one is a spectator; all are participants. As Segal shows in his summary of findings,[9] there were times in the history of Israel when in the celebration of the Passover worshippers did become more like spectators. The ritual was formalized and centralized. Yet even then there was always a strong element of participation by each household. My experience of Easter in Athens in the year 2000 helped me to appreciate how the members of the Greek Orthodox Church have retained this feature of the celebration. In the Easter ritual at the Midnight Eucharist all members of the community took their candles to be lit from the Paschal Candle in the church and in candle-light passed along the streets and paths to return home, there to partake in the feast of the lamb roasted over the spit. The worship of the church and the home was united in the remembrance of new life brought to us through the resurrection of Christ.

In the Passover account there is a place for active symbols: the removal of the leaven to denote purity, the wearing of appropriate dress, the preparation of the right foods, the identification with the people of God, the rehearsal of the story in answer to the question from the representative of the next generation. All this is linked to memory and the creation of memory. God is present because of the past, and God is affirmed as protective of the future. Memory and worship link arms to express the ongoing relationship between the worshipper and God. We remember to worship, and worship to remember who God is and what God has done. The stimuli of taste, smell, and sight evoke memories and create memories. Such

---

[8]   Houtman (1996) p. 144.
[9]   Segal (1963, pp. 266–8.

worship involves both the community and the individual so that the experience of the one flows into the experience of the other. God is seen as the creator, the provider, the redeemer, the enabler, the protector from despair, and the purpose of the future. As the worshipper participates in such liturgy the question is evoked: 'What does this mean for us, for me, now, at this Passover, at this time, in this context, and for the future?' Each year the ritual is repeated so we know where we are and who we are from the familiar pattern. The past comes alive and enables new experiences of the divine and a deeper relationship with God.

When you examine my seven points listed above they are seen to be fully illustrated in this pattern of Passover worship. For Christians, Holy Week liturgies can create similar patterns. The constant symbols of redemption and resurrection provoke the memories and create memories on which true worship is based. In a later chapter I will discuss the issues of stability and novelty in worship, but clearly here I want to stress the obvious: that such Christian worship needs to aim at full participation, at the involvement of all the senses, and the constancy of the main symbols.

The Creed

When we speak of remembering God it is right that we should include reference to the place of the Creed in worship. Within the Christian Church the various creeds have figured prominently in worship even though their purpose has been given differing explanations from time to time.[10]

A creed is a statement of what the Church has come to believe about the nature and purpose of God. A creed is the badge we claim that identifies us as belonging to a wide family of Christian peoples, constituted now and in the past There have been creeds incorporated in Christian worship from earliest times, from simple statements such as 'Jesus is Lord' to the fuller statements of what this might mean for Christian people. These creeds arise from struggles to define the truth. What is known as the 'Old Roman Creed' was an earlier and shorter form of that now-entitled the Apostles' Creed. The Roman Creed is found in the Apostolic Traditions of Hippolytus (c. AD 235), and in other literature from the fourth century. It appears likely that such a simple creed was in use in the Church in Rome from about the end of the second century.

A fuller version of such a creed grew in prominence in later centuries in association with the Baptismal rite. The Apostles' Creed is based on the pattern of the Trinity foreshadowed in Matthew 28:19. In the form of words we now have in our liturgy it was first quoted by an eighth-century writer in western Christendom. By the early Middle Ages it was in common use in the West as a baptismal creed, and its use was incorporated into the pattern of daily services soon after that. Its treasure for us is the link between regular worship and our Baptism, which keeps us within the context of faith in God in Trinity.

The history of the Nicene Creed is even more complex. This creed evolved out

---

[10] See the chapter on 'Creed', in Kenneth Stevenson (2002), *Do This*, p. 102ff.

of the struggle of the church to define what was 'orthodox', that is, agreed as regular or correct. This struggle, often bitter and full of power politics, was a long one, and concentrated on rejecting heresy rather than on what individuals might find helpful as a statement of belief in the context of worship. These creedal statements were to be seen as boundary markers. The struggle to formulate the words started at the Council held at Nicaea in AD 325, developed further at the Council of Constantinople in AD 381, and then at the Council of Chalcedon in AD 451. Further minor changes were made in the following centuries. In the end this creed found its way into the Liturgy of the Eucharist as a sign that the Church that included it belonged to the family of Christian churches which saw itself as having the 'correct' interpretation of the Faith.

Professor Averil Cameron, a renowned historian, has this to say about the use of the Creed in liturgy:

> In saying the Creed, the modern worshipper assents to the collective history and the current and future community of the Church as the bearer of orthodoxy. He or she may think he is describing his own beliefs but actually he/she is associating himself as a member of the Christian group.[11]

In saying the Creed (whichever one is in that order of liturgy) the worshipper is identifying with the whole community of the Church. Professor Cameron rightly adds these words of warning:

> An important function of the liturgy is to preserve memory, the collective memory of the Church, and this applies in large measure to the creed. The danger, though, is that most of us have forgotten what that memory really relates to.[12]

Dropping the Creed in the Liturgy only accentuates the dislocation of memory. If this continues we will soon be unable to remember who we are and in whom we believe. The worshipper may remember that 'Jesus is Lord' but not be able to remember the breadth of the relationship with God in God's plenitude. In any relationship the parties need to remember who they are, how they are related, and what is the purpose of the relationship. The Creeds, however much they were born out of a struggle and are imperfect as to language, have stood the test of time to be the best available expression of our corporate faith. As Professor Cameron puts it:

> The Creed is a badge of identity. It marks us off, and it stakes a claim, just as it did when it was first composed. For all its faults and curiosities, it is the outward symbol of unity, used by churches not unified in other respects.[13]

There is value in committing the words of the Creed to familiarity if not to full memory. With a little understanding of its phrases it provides us with a sense that in worship we honour a God we have bothered to get to know as far as we can put

---

[11] Cameron, Averil (2001), 'The Creed', in Stephen Conway (ed.), *Living the Eucharist*, p. 60.
[12] Cameron (2001), p. 68.
[13] Cameron (2001), p. 68.

that knowledge into words. Such an effort will constantly remind us that God is more than we can define, yet one who has graced us with a revelation of enough of the divine nature to make the relationship fruitful. The Creed calls to mind our baptism and our commitment to God. The memory of the words helps us to keep fresh the 'symbol' of God in the fullness of a word picture. The recitation of the Creed allows us to grasp who we are and who God is, and to whom we belong. As always the memory of the outwards words will cause the mind to stretch itself to discover more of the boundaries of our knowledge of God, and encourage us to search for the fullness of life and meaning in this world and in resurrection.

Remembering God

Above all activities, worship provides us with the opportunity to remember God, to recall the relationship between us and to recapture that sense of belonging and value that restores us to harmony and humility which are the hallmarks of true humanity. Worship, through memory, links us to the past, affirms us in the present, and gives us cause to reflect on the way ahead in the company of the Divine Spirit. To remember God brings us into our true place and potential in the created order and enables us to be in harmony, full *shalom*, with God and all things.

Chapter 4

God's Memory of Us

God's Initiative – Our Identity

The last chapter showed how remembrance of God forms the foundation of all our worship. To remember God is to recall all aspects of our relationship with God, to touch again those experiences which are significant and meaningful for us, and to give them renewed life. Yet if we are not careful we will fall into the trap of thinking that God only exists if we retain a conscious memory of God. With the fashionable focus on the human individual, some are tempted to think that God becomes alive when the human mind makes it its pleasure to remember God. Yet Scripture bears witness that it is God who takes the initiative in the relationship with humanity.[1] Acknowledging the priority of God allows us to say 'God remembers us.' To think in these terms is to give inspiration to our relationship with God through worship and to establish our true identity. Who I am is the result, not of my own initiative and invention, but of God's purpose for each one as a member of the human race and as individuals within it. Liturgically it is in the sacrament of Baptism that we discover this identity and this purpose for our lives.

In 1980 William Willimon wrote a book with the revealing title *Remember Who You Are: Baptism, a Model of Christian Life*.[2] Willimon is clear that baptism is essentially something which God does and to which we respond, rather than our action to which God is gracious enough to respond. These two quotations summarize Willimon's thesis:

> We are who we are because [God] has loved us, chosen us, adopted us, anointed us for his own.[3]

> Through baptism, a Christian first and finally learns who he or she is. It is the rite of identity.[4]

For Willimon a key Biblical reference for baptism is that recorded in 1 Peter 2:9:

---

[1] This is not only clear from the creation narratives in Genesis chapter 1 and 2 but also in the writings of John: 1 John 4:19 'We love because he first loved us' and 1 John 3:1 'See what love the Father has given us, that we should be called children of God.' John 3:16, a key verse in John's Gospel, clearly shows God's initiative: 'For God so loved the world that he gave his only Son, so that everyone who believes in him may not perish but may have eternal life.'

[2] William H. Willimon (1980), *Remember Who You Are: Baptism, a Model for Christian Life*.

[3] Ibid., p. 28.

[4] Ibid., p. 27.

But you are a chosen race, a royal priesthood, a holy nation, God's own people, that you may declare the wonderful deeds of him who called you out of darkness into his marvelous light.

This verse signifies that in the act of baptism we are grafted into the vine of Christ to become the new people of God, and that our individuality is incorporated into the community which holds firm to the memory of the presence of Christ, and which knows who it is and what it is called to do. In the Christian community memory and mission intertwine and become effective.

Called by Name

Most of us are aware of our identity as a person when we hear our name called. It is our name which seems to capture who we are – our personhood, even our personality. In many cultures the name given to a person creates links with the past. We are named after some ancestor, relative or family friend who has already filled the name with a sense of honour. For a Christian the name may have already belonged to a saint of the Church, and for us to hold it as 'our' name bestows on us both an honour and a responsibility. The name links us to our new family, the Christian community of this and of all generations. Our name is our identity, by which we are known for good or evil. It is interesting to note that in many official documents we are asked to record a 'family' name and a 'given' name. The implication is that we did not choose our name but that it was given to us. It was a gift that declared we were a precious person, the object of love and respect. The name was ours before we were conscious of it. By our name we remember our identity, and others know us for who we are.

These words from one of the prophets connect the concept of being called by name with the actions which take place at baptism:

> . . . Thus says the Lord . . . do not fear,
> for I have redeemed you,
> I have called you by name,
> you are mine.
> When you pass through the waters,
> I will be with you;
> and through the rivers,
> they shall not overwhelm you;
> when you walk through fire
> you shall not be burned,
> and the flame shall not consume you.
> For I am the Lord your God,
> the Holy One of Israel, your Savior.[5]

---

[5] Isa. 43:1–3 selected portions.

For those called by name, the waters of baptism are a watershed when the old life of selfishness is drowned, evil is consumed by fire,[6] and the action of God for our redemption is displayed.

In the Gospels the concept of being known by God by name is evidenced in John's description of Jesus as the Good Shepherd who 'calls his own sheep by name and leads them out'.[7] The relationship between the sheep and the shepherd is so intimate that the precious nature of each sheep is symbolized and recalled by the sense that each is worthy of a name. Such a sheep is not a 'thing' of little value in its own right, but a part of creation which is precious to God. The point of the parable is to highlight the relationship between God and humanity. John's Gospel follows through on this insight by the way a person's name is used in two key passages referring to the new life of resurrection. Jesus addresses the brother of Mary and Martha by his name 'Lazarus' as Jesus calls him forth from the tomb.[8] In the Easter garden Jesus addresses Mary by her name to enable her to recall the relationship with her Lord.[9] By the use of the personal name, Jesus brings to life the relationship which exists between the person and himself, a relationship not even death can break.

Because they expressed the relationship between God and each baptized disciple, names in the life of the early Church became so precious that the idea arose that the names of those who shared in resurrection would be recorded on a scroll. The writer of the Epistle to the Philippians greets 'My co-workers, whose names are in the book of life'.[10] Such language is found in greater detail in the Book of Revelation:

> If you conquer, you will be clothed like them in white robes, and I will not blot your name out of the book of life; I will confess your name before my Father and before his angels.[11]

Here we also note the links between baptism (the white robe put on the newly baptized), and the concept of each disciple having a given name. God's memory of us is embodied in a name by which we are known to God, and by which we come to remember who we are as a person.

Baptism

In baptism we acquire our name and our character as a Christian. Both are given to us by God through the ministry of the Church. In baptism the Church declares God's memory of us and God's mission for us. In baptism we first receive and then respond. We hear our name and accept the responsibility of living up to who

---

6 Compare Matt. 3:11 and Luke 3:16.
7 John 10:3.
8 John 11:43.
9 John 20:16.
10 Phil. 4:3.
11 Rev. 3:15.

we are. The fact that baptism is the initiative of God and thus of the Church was made clear in the widespread practice of baptizing people of all ages. Infants were included wherever the unit of the Christian family was established. In missionary situations, where the challenge of the Gospel for repentance is accepted by some and rejected by others, the likelihood is that only those of mature years will be judged ready to receive baptism. The test must always be readiness to receive rather than confidence in the amount of faith and knowledge displayed. The history of baptism records how the Church has staggered between the poles of how much to concentrate on God's grace and how much on the human response at the time of baptism.

James White has summarized the various positions in his recent book *The Sacraments in Protestant Practice*.[12] Though he writes of the position since the Reformation, White highlights the continuing polarity of views. Luther's position was that 'Baptism remains as a lifelong assurance that "I am baptized, and through my baptism God, who cannot lie, has bound himself in a covenant with me."' So the Christian life is a 'continual remembrance of the promise made to us in baptism'.[13]

Among other Christians, especially in parts of the United States, this position was eroded by a new view that baptism was the occasion, not for the activity of God but for the affirmation of the faith of the individual believer. It was the time for a testimony that 'I have discovered God and am ready to declare my faith.' So the emphasis was on the believer and the strength of their faith and commitment. The name given to this viewpoint was 'Believer's baptism' in contrast to 'Infant baptism', with the implication that infants could not have faith in God in their own right, and that it is faith which creates the right conditions for baptism. In such a view baptism is an individual, not a corporate, activity. As White says: 'Believer's baptism was simply a sign of faith to which an individual could give his or her own testimony. Anything supernatural was firmly located in biblical times and not the present.'[14]

I have no doubt that the debate will continue to divide the Church. The missionary situations are continually changing and demand different emphases. Yet at all times it is vital to recapture the sense of the priority of God's grace and the corporate faith that God does act in baptism out of love for those baptized, whatever age they happen to be. The key consideration in this chapter is the way that baptism helps us to keep in mind God's memory of us, and in that recollection provides us with the strength and grace to live as disciples of Christ.

Five Metaphors for Baptism

White has set out five metaphors for baptism as recorded in the New Testament:

---

[12] James F. White (1999), *The Sacraments in Protestant Practice*.
[13] Ibid., p. 34.
[14] Ibid., p. 39.

- forgiveness of sin
- union with Christ, especially his death and resurrection
- incorporation into the Church
- reception of the Holy Spirit
- new birth or regeneration.[15]

Each of these metaphors deals with an ongoing situation. Therefore our memory of our baptism is not so much of a past event but of a current status. It is more important for Christians to remember that they are baptized than the date and method of their baptism. It is true that our status now does rely on an event that happened in the past. However the key memory is of the ongoing relationship we have with God because of that past event. The metaphors help us remember our current situation. As we look at each in turn this will become more evident.

Forgiveness of Sin

When I am aware of my sinfulness I need to find a way to deal with that knowledge before I become frozen in guilt or hardened into making excuses or denials. The assurance that forgiveness is possible and that to seek it is appropriate provides the antidote to sin. Such an assurance allows a person to acknowledge sinfulness, seek forgiveness and strive for reconciliation and restitution. This assurance comes from the declaration of forgiveness that God made at baptism. Water has the quality of washing things clean whenever it is used. So the promise of forgiveness that God gives at baptism not only cleanses sin at that moment, but shows God's nature is to be forgiving whenever in the future the baptized repents of sin and seeks forgiveness. Too often the debate in the Church has been about the nature of the sinfulness of the person at the point of baptism, and the possibility of being forgiven after baptism. To limit God's forgiveness would be similar to holding the view that Christ's act of salvation on the Cross was only effective for the sins of those who repented on the day of crucifixion. This is not the teaching or the experience of the Church. It is widely agreed that the Cross is effective as the means of bringing people in touch with Christ's salvation at every point in history. If that position is accepted it would seem right to see baptism as the promise of ongoing forgiveness for all occasions when sin and repentance occur. The waters of baptism are a continual fountain of cleansing so that there is always an experience of being forgiven and renewed to live a life of reconciliation with God and neighbour. White declares:

> Throughout life, we can recall with hope that we have been forgiven in baptism . . . Baptism is the real sacrament of penance, and throughout life we can take consolation in the cleansing we have received in Christ's blood in baptism.[16]

---

[15] Ibid., p. 53.
[16] Ibid., p. 57.

Union to Christ

Saint Paul wrote to the Church in Rome of his experience of baptism:

> Do you not know that all of us who have been baptized into Christ Jesus were baptized
> into his death? . . . For if we have been united with him in a death like his, we will
> certainly be united with him in a resurrection like his.[17]

To be united to Christ is both to share in his victory over sin and death and to
share in his mission to the world. In the midst of trial and tribulation it is vital to
recall that Christ has triumphed over all kinds of death, and opened for the baptized
access to life eternal. To die with Christ at baptism is a death more significant even
than our mortal death. When we remember that eternal life began at our baptism,
we will be able at our death to die with a sure and certain hope that we share in
the resurrection. Living in this constant memory gives us new power to deal with
the suffering we endure in the world around us. We are remembered by God as
those whom Christ claims as his own. Knowing this we will have no fear that we
will not be strong enough to face the rigors of life, even of death. Through baptism
we are also united to the Christ who intercedes for us and for the world. As the
baptized people of God we share in this victory through prayer and add our
spiritual strength to the work of Christ's intercession.

This metaphor of baptism is highlighted in the question and response which
concludes the presentation of a person for baptism in the baptismal liturgy in the
New Zealand Prayer Book.

> *Question*: Do you trust in Christ's victory which brings forgiveness, freedom and life?
> *Response*: In faith I turn to Christ, my way, my truth, my life.[18]

Later in this chapter under practical considerations I will expand on ways that
baptism and the renewal of the baptismal covenant at the Paschal festival can
provide the means to keep fresh the fact that God remembers us through baptism
as those who are united to Christ in his death and resurrection. Such a unity is also
affirmed on the occasion of each Eucharist as the baptized worshipper witnesses
and experiences unity with Christ at the reception of the sacramental bread and
wine.

Incorporation into the Church

Baptism unites us with Christ and therefore with the body of Christ, the Church.
One of the myths of modern society is that the individual is more important than
the community. This has caused some people to feel that they can choose whether
or not to be linked up with their human family, or the family of the Church. For
such people the obligations of both human and Church family are taken up or put
down at the desire of the individual. This is unnatural (against the 'nature' and

---

[17] Rom. 6:3 and 5.
[18] NZPB (1989) p. 385.

inherent principle) in both instances. By nature of our birth we are gifted life from a human family. No individual can ask to be born into a particular family; he or she can only accept (or reject) the gift of belonging. To reject such a gift only leaves individuals constantly anxious about who they are and to whom they belong. This anxiety replaces the memory of giftedness and incorporation. The parallel can be applied to the adoption of a member into the family of the Church through baptism. Jesus clearly understood the need for Christians to have a sense of belonging to a new family made up of those who were his disciples.[19] Jesus foresaw that baptism could cut disciples off from a natural family whose other members rejected the truth he revealed. Jesus even experienced alienation from his own family for a while. Thus he gathered around himself a new family, a community of mutual love, support and forgiveness. Through this community the love of God for each person would be experienced and shared. God's memory of us was made real as the new family of the Church knew and respected each member by a special name, their Christian name. This deep sense of fellowship (sharing all things in common) was seen as a key gift of God's Spirit. It was baptism that promised and provided this gift and therefore gave entrance to this gifted community. Without the mutual support of the community the baptized would soon fall from grace. The baptized would no longer experience what it meant to be forgiven, how to pray with Christ, how to share, and how to live the way of Christ. The point is well made in these words of the congregation addressed to those who have just received the waters of baptism in the name of the Trinity:

> God receives you by baptism into the Church.
> Child of God, blessed in the Spirit,
> welcome to the family of Christ.[20]

The presence of significant members of the Church community at every baptism is a vital witness to this metaphor of baptism. For a relatively short time in western civilization baptism became a 'family affair' in the wrong sense of that phrase. Only the human family and their friends were present with the candidate and the priest. For a time it was possible for them to represent the Church family because they were almost one and the same. As the division between citizenship and Church membership took place so the concept of the natural family as equal to the Church family at baptism lapsed. Today the Church is very aware of that division and has stressed once more the need at a baptism to show the newly baptized the members of their new family. In the New Zealand liturgy of baptism a place is made for a representative of the congregation to present a lighted candle to the newly baptized with the words:

> Walk in the faith of Christ,
> crucified and risen,
> shine with the light of Christ.[21]

---

[19] Mark 3:31–35, Matt. 12:46, Luke 8:19.
[20] NZPB (1989), p. 386.
[21] NZPB (1989), p. 387.

Where the Church community appoints a guardian for the newly baptized to encourage growth in faith and mission, it will be appropriate for that guardian to present the candle and maintain the link through that symbol in years to come. The candle becomes an ongoing remembrance of the occasion of baptism, and who presented it and why it was given.

Above all, the community of faith continually reaffirms to those baptized that God has a memory for each of them. As White has shown, the prominence of the baptismal font in the place of worship can assist every member to keep the memory of baptism afresh. He writes 'Baptism is the sign-act of entrance into the church and hence fonts are often placed at the doors of churches.'[22] For example as you enter the cathedral of the Catholic Diocese of Assisi in Umbria you will have pointed out to you on the right of the entrance the font in which both Saint Francis and Saint Clare were baptized as infants. Its substantial presence reminds us all that there is somewhere a font, or bath, or basin, or river in which we were baptized and made a member of the Church. This Church is not simply local; rather it is universal, linking every place and generation. Baptism is our gift of being held in the memory of God and the whole Christian community.

Reception of the Holy Spirit

The Acts of the Apostles records an address by Saint Peter on the Day of Pentecost. In it he states that in baptism 'you will receive the gift of the Holy Spirit'.[23] However in later chapters of the same book the record of the early Church shows that the Spirit was bestowed according to a variety of patterns. Sometimes the gift came before baptism,[24] sometimes it came in association with the laying on of hands separate from baptism,[25] and sometimes it is accompanied with particular gifts such as speaking with tongues and healing.[26] What seems to have been 'regular' is that we can expect the action of baptism to be the occasion when the promise of the gift of the Holy Spirit is fulfilled. This is the experience recorded for Saint Paul in Acts 9:17–19, and to which he gives his own testimony in his writings about life in the Spirit.[27] The statement that we are given the Holy Spirit at baptism does not prevent us also receiving the gift at another time for some specific purpose to fulfill our mission. There is a parallel here between the forgiveness of sin at baptism and God's promise to go on forgiving us whenever we seek it through repentance. That the Spirit is given at baptism does not prevent God giving us the appropriate gift as an outworking of that promise on future occasions. However to deny that God does give us the gift of Godself in the Spirit at baptism is to restrict the Godhead to two persons at baptism. If we are baptized in the name of the Trinity, then all the persons of the Godhead must be present and

---

[22]   White (1999), p. 61.
[23]   Acts 2:38.
[24]   Acts 10:47.
[25]   Acts 8:14–16.
[26]   Acts 4:29–31.
[27]   Rom. 8:1–17.

active in our baptism. For God to remember us through baptism means we relate to the whole of God – Father, Son and Holy Spirit. That is the witness of the Church, and that is the witness of Christians who can recognize God at work in a variety of ways on a variety of occasions throughout their Christian life.

To speak of a baptism in the Spirit which is not associated with water is to conjoin words in a way that does violence to Scripture and Theology. Baptism is always in water in the name of the Trinity – the Spirit included. The experience of the gift of the Spirit is real enough, both in Scripture and the continuing experience of the Church. It may be associated with the laying on of hands for service, lay or ordained; or for the gift of healing; or for the gift of reconciliation and renewal. A gift of the Spirit may be received in a time of prayer and waiting upon God. However the fundamental gift of the Spirit is essential for fellowship within the Church, for the regular life of prayer and ministry, and for the witness and testimony to the faith we hold in common. Those gifts are essential in every baptized member of the Church, and without those gifts baptism would be fruitless. The Church prays for the newly baptized:

> May you grow in the Holy Spirit,
> fulfill your ministry,
> and follow Christ your whole life long.[28]

Our memory of being baptized assures us that we do indeed have the gifts of the Spirit that enable us to be disciples of Christ. To be united to Christ also means that we are empowered by his Spirit through baptism.

New Birth or Regeneration

Controversy has also surrounded this metaphor for baptism. There is a natural link between a candidate rising up from the waters of baptism and our birth from the waters of the womb. The Scriptures speak of being 'raised with Christ' in baptism.[29] The writer of the Epistle to the Colossians links being raised with 'being renewed in knowledge according to the image of its creator'.[30] The life of a baptized Christian was felt to be so new that it was like a rebirth. Such an image appeals to those who point out that Scripture contains feminine metaphors as well as masculine ones, with which the Church has more readily identified. White comments: 'So the metaphor of new birth is in process of being rediscovered. As one of the most explicitly feminine images in all of Scripture, it can help balance overwhelmingly masculine imagery.'[31]

The controversy arises because the key verse in John's Gospel: 'No one can enter the kingdom of God without being born of water and spirit'[32] has been

---

[28] NZPB (1989), p. 389.
[29] Col. 3:12 'When you were buried with him in baptism, you were also raised with him through faith in the power of God, who raised him from the dead.'
[30] Col. 3:10.
[31] White (1999), p. 70.
[32] John 3:5.

'captured' by those who experience the inner conversion of the soul as the key experience in becoming a follower of Christ. For such people to be born again is a matter of the soul rather than the whole person. For some of those who were baptized as infants and cannot mark any response to date on their part, an act of soul conversion is experienced as a first entry into the kingdom. They have no memory of baptism as having significance or meaning, so they assume that God has had no memory of them until they were conscious of God's power in their lives. Being limited in their experience of God, they limit God's experience of them. That the verse in John's Gospel mentions water as well as spirit only provokes such people to ask for 'proper' baptism. They want an experience in which they fully share, and one which fulfills certain criteria such as the correct amount of water, or total immersion, or the correct amount of faith and repentance. When the Church community, in which some people experience this rebirth of the soul, forgets that baptism is the declaration of God's memory of us and God's promise of ongoing life and love, and sets forth some other teaching, then it is difficult for those 'reborn' not to follow the instructions as to what is necessary.

At our natural birth we experience new life without being fully conscious of it until a later date. So hopefully we will see the new life from baptism as one which, by the work of the Spirit of God, we become more and more aware and respond accordingly. In our natural life as we grow to maturity there are many steps when we declare 'Now I see!' with enthusiasm and joy. This does not indicate that we were unable to see at all beforehand. The gift of sight has always been ours. Rather we proclaim 'Now I can see!' when a new truth fits into the pattern of understanding for which our brain searches. The metaphor equally applies to the life of faith and the journey of understanding who God is and what God has done for us.

In the light of this ongoing controversy it seems vital that baptismal liturgies make clear that the waters of baptism are indeed the waters of rebirth. Here is an example:

We thank you that through the waters of baptism
you cleanse us,
renew us by your Spirit
and raise us to new life.

In the new covenant
we are made members of your Church
and share in your eternal kingdom.

Through your Holy Spirit
fulfill once more your promises
in this water of rebirth,
set apart in the name of our Lord Jesus Christ.[33]

---

[33] NZPB (1989), p. 386.

Re-baptism

The whole concept of re-baptism can now be seen as a misunderstanding of the actions of baptism. God is the one who at our baptism takes the initiative and declares that we are:

> children of God,
> called by name,
> members of the whole Christian community,

and therefore,

> sealed as prophets, priests and kings,
> united in Christ,
> gifted with the Spirit,
> raised to new life,
> born for ever into the kingdom.

This action of God cannot be denied. God's promises cannot be undone. Our response may falter, and needs to be renewed. We may even seek to forget God; but God does not forget us.

To call for re-baptism for whatever reason is to cast doubt on God's ability to act. And if we do this once, why not again and again? A re-baptism can only add to any anxiety that we are not worthy of baptism, or have not fulfilled the right details, or that God failed to give us the promised gifts. As we shall see shortly, we do need help to keep alive the memory of baptism and this will require opportunities for reaffirmation and renewal, but NOT for a further baptism. God has given us a new name and it is ours for ever, in this life and eternity.

Spiritual Amnesia

Laurence Stookey defined the condition of so many Christians as having spiritual amnesia: 'Each of us suffers from spiritual amnesia. We forget what God has done for us and promised to us. In short, we are oblivious to the identity we have been given by our Creator.'[34] He points out that our remembrance of the connection with water helps to counteract this amnesia and that baptism and our witness to it puts us in constant touch with water:

> Through the water of baptism, God brings to our remembrance the stories of the early Chapters of Genesis ... The stories of creation presented to us through the water of baptism bring to our attention central themes of the gospel that enable us to know who we are – and whose we are.[35]

---

[34] Laurence H. Stookey (1982), *Baptism – Christ's Act in the Church*, p. 13.
[35] Ibid.

Through the water of baptism, God brings to our attention the covenant made with Noah after the flood . . . [and] of the covenant with Israel, which was accompanied by many events involving water.[36]

These links, through water, with creation and covenant help establish in the believer and the community the memory of God's initiatives and human responsibility. They lead us to the water of the baptism of Christ and to the water at the baptism of this liturgical act: 'Baptism is itself a covenant God initiates with us; the water is the sign given to us to help us remember the promise of the Lord, and to remind us of our identity as a responsible people.'[37]

In Chapters 1 and 2 of this book I have noted how memory works best when links join one event or knowledge with others in a chain-like cord. The use of the common substance water allows the memory to make constant connections. Because water is so common in the story of life and the story of God's actions and memory of us as an ongoing people of God, water can evoke and recapture the experience and knowledge we have of God. It is sad that the modern tendency is to separate the sacred from the secular, thereby loosening the connection between water in creation and water in baptism. It is part of the cause of our spiritual amnesia. If we can reconnect our memories then we will find it easier to retain the memory of being baptized with its assurance of God's memory of us. Every time we wash in water we will recall with thanksgiving the God who offers to cleanse us from all sin. Every time we see plants sustained by the water of creation we will recall how the Spirit of God sustains our growth to spiritual maturity. Every time we behold the sparkling water in a river we will remember Christ's baptism and his experience of the Spirit in the waters of the Jordan. Every time we hear of a drowning we will consider with seriousness the need to die to sin and rise to righteousness. When the waters are broken and a baby enters new life, we will rejoice in our continual renewal in life in the power of God, who has quickened us to life eternal. Every time we drink a refreshing cup of cold water, we will know that we are renewed with spiritual energy for the mission and ministry of the kingdom of God, and at the same time recognize the needs of Christ in those who are thirsty, spiritually and materially.

When the Spirit of God helps us to make such connections we will overcome our difficulty remembering our baptismal status. Instead the memories will come 'flooding' back to sustain, refresh and cleanse us. Stookey declares:

Nothing in creation has the power to remind us so fully of the work of our Lord as the common substance of water. This he gives us at baptism as a token of his saving grace, so that from the time of our initiation onward we may be reminded of all he has done for us, so that we may see ourselves as a people united to him and to one another in him.[38]

---

[36] Ibid., p. 14.
[37] Ibid., p. 15.
[38] Ibid., p. 16.

Keeping the Memory Alive

The mind retains material to be remembered when the experience or knowledge is significant, regularly recalled, linked by association with other material, and where it fits into the framework of other belief patterns, accepted knowledge and experience. It is one of the functions of liturgy to assist the brain to retain the memory and apply its significance to the actions in life. In the light of this information it is important now to see how the liturgies associated with the sacrament of baptism and any renewal of its meaning can be conducted in such a way as to assist the retention and application of this vital memory. Let us examine two key principles and a range of more detailed practical suggestions.

The *first principle* is that the liturgical service of baptism should be held regularly in the midst of each congregation at least four times in a year. These services should be held at a time and place when the greatest representation of all the members of the congregation can be present. The purpose of these services is not simply to baptize those candidates of whatever age who have been presented and prepared since the last occasion for baptism. It is also to allow every Christian present to call to mind their own baptism and what God did then and does now for God's children. If on any set occasion there are no candidates for baptism (which seems unlikely in most congregations) then a service of the renewal of the baptismal covenant should take place as part of the liturgy of the day. The absence of candidates should be seen as an incentive for greater zeal in mission and nurture during the next quarter of the year.

The *second principle* is that a service of renewal of the baptismal covenant should be included in the Easter programme. For some traditions such a service is held early on the eve of Easter. Others will deem it appropriate as part of the festival on Easter Day or on the first Sunday in the Octave. In this service the focus should be on God's activity through baptism as well as our acceptance of our privileges and responsibilities. The five metaphors of baptism should provide the themes for such a liturgy.[39]

---

[39]   The following verses and responses are a new composition by the author, and may be used and adapted without the need to seek his further permission:

Blessed be God who through baptism calls each of us by name.
   We are baptized in the name of God: the Father, the Son, and the Holy Spirit.
Blessed be God who through baptism declares forgiveness for our sins.
   We are baptized into the river of forgiveness which sweeps away our sins.
Blessed be God who through baptism unites us with Christ.
   Through baptism we have been buried with Christ and raised with him to life eternal.
Blessed be God who through baptism makes us members of the church.
   We are bound together in the fellowship of the Spirit as the people of God, the prophet and priest of God's kingdom.
Blessed be God who through baptism has filled us with the Holy Spirit.
   We are empowered by the Spirit's grace to live in faith, and strive for peace and justice.

In addition to these two principles there are a range of practical suggestions for those who conduct the liturgy of baptism. The aim of these suggestions is to enable the baptized to remember who they are and to whom they belong.

- The evidence of water must be clearly visible and significant within a liturgy of baptism. Water should be poured into the bath or basin during the thanksgiving prayer. Both the sound and the sight of the water are vital triggers for memory. The amount of water used for the baptism must be enough for the people involved to become wet. Those being baptized should feel the water and the sensation of being wet. This can be achieved by using a shell large enough to hold a volume of water which can then be poured over the candidate, even where full immersion is not preferred or practical. At every baptism a full-sized towel will be required and this provides a good test as to whether a memorable amount of water has been used.

- During a renewal of the baptismal covenant it is helpful to have the font or bath filled with water so that the congregation can return to the symbolic place of baptism to sprinkle themselves again with water, or make the sign of the cross on themselves with the water. The baptized themselves can take responsibility for being in touch with the waters of baptism. There should be no sense in which the priest is seen as 're-baptizing' the congregation by sprinkling them with water. It is also important that the title of any service for this purpose should be the Renewal of the Baptismal Covenant, not the Renewal of Baptismal Vows. The latter title calls attention only to the human response in baptism and not also to the ongoing memory of God's grace.

- Some churches make certain that the baptismal ewer (or other water container) is kept visible at the altar during the liturgy of the Eucharist. This reminds the congregation that there is a clear link between the two sacraments. Those baptized into the Body of Christ are able to share the Body of Christ as revealed in the bread and wine of the Eucharist. The significance of this symbolism will need to be reaffirmed by the celebrant at regular intervals throughout the year. It is also proper for the Eucharist to follow a service of Baptism and for those just baptized to receive their communion.

- The Paschal Candle will be used at the font on all occasions when there is a baptism so that the link with Christ's death and resurrection is visibly displayed. The candle given to the newly baptized should be lit from this Paschal Candle.

- Some churches provide a 'holy stoop' filled with fresh water at the entrance to the church. Members of these congregations dip their fingers in the water and make the sign of the cross. The following words may be suitable to use

---

Blessed be God who through baptism has given us birth to newness of life.
We are born again by water and the Spirit to share in the work of the kingdom.
Blessed be God who through baptism remembers us and establishes a covenant with us.
We give thanks to our God and dedicate our lives anew to God's glory.

with such a custom: 'I am a disciple of Christ, baptized in the name of the Father, and of the Son, and of the Holy Spirit.'

- Oil can be used for the assignation of the newly baptized. This oil of chrism is usually pure olive oil perfumed with scent to express the joy of baptism and the foretaste of heaven. The use of this oil for making the sign of the cross after baptism avoids any misunderstanding that the purpose of water in baptism is to mark the sign of the cross on the forehead of the baptized. When oil is used at the baptism, the anointing can later be linked to the preparation for the entry through mortal death into life eternal. The association may be retained by using suitable words at the anointing before death:

> N . . ., you have been buried with Christ in baptism and raised to newness of life. Again we anoint you with this holy oil. Christ keep you in eternal life, and bring you safely to the joys of heaven. Go on your journey in peace, and rest in God's everlasting care.[40]

- The recitation of the Creed in services of worship is a constant reminder of the act of faith declared at baptism. Where the ordinances allow, those leading worship may use one of the familiar statements of faith affirmed during a liturgy of baptism as the Creed or its substitute at a regular service of worship. The connection and purpose of the use should be drawn to the attention of the congregation from time to time.

- Where infants and young children are included among the candidates for baptism it is important that the church provides ongoing occasions for them to call to mind their baptism. At least once a year a short service should be held so that they can gather at the font. One of the various aspects and qualities of water should form the focus of such a service. In later years they should be specially invited to participate in the annual renewal of the baptismal covenant at a time which marks an age of first responsibility (about 9 to 11 years) and later again with greater maturity (about 16 to 19 years). If the practice of Confirmation is continued, then the basic experience of baptism should be in evidence both in symbol and word. The young people on these occasions should be encouraged to bring their baptismal certificate or candle with them.

All these practical suggestions are made to enhance the memory's ability to keep fresh the acknowledgment of the status of being baptized. Without opportunities to be in touch with the fact of our baptism, the memory of who we are will fade away, only to be recalled in some crisis or in a fresh experience of the grace of God. Our memories need ongoing prompting for us to hold fast to the actions of God on our behalf. As we face the trials of life it is good to remember that

---

[40] Original verses by the author; may be used without further permission.

'Baptism is a gift from Christ that can overcome our tendency to forget the hope we have in him and in his final triumph over sin and death.'[41]

The primary purpose of our baptism is to establish that God remembers us as those known by name and claimed as part of God's own people, called to honour and serve the divine will and purpose.

---

[41] Stookey (1982), p. 17.

Chapter 5

Remembering Jesus Christ

Remembering a Person

Think of the process that takes place when we remember someone well known to us. When we remember such a person our brain makes connections with a set of stored data: events, actions, words and physical features. It also connects with a set of stored feelings and emotions: joy, sadness, inspiration, comfort, strength and maybe regrets, which that person stirred up in us and maybe still stirs up in us because of the depth of our relationship. Our memory is able to link data with feelings to recreate in the present a sense of relationship with that person, and all that it means for us. Thinking about the process we can see the truth of these words by Jim Cotter: 'To re-member is to re-embody, to bring together, to bring alive, that which is past, and to make it effective in the present and for the future.'[1]

When we remember a person, the brain sets up a process which is circular. Feelings for the person remembered connect with data about that person, and these in turn connect with current feelings about the relationship. These in turn affect the way we conduct our lives in the future.[2] Our feelings about a person can create a picture in the mind which helps the mind focus on the data which is most significant for the relationship. Stories about actions undertaken by the person remembered will become focused on a few key details. Memories of spoken words will be focused on the main point to retain, and may hinge on a key phrase or illustration. Memories about a key event may be focused by the place in which the event took place. A place or object can be retained in the memory and it in turn evokes a current set of feelings. One memory can cause a link with a further memory to create a strong chain of connected memories of that person.

Through the faculty of memory the person remembered can 'come alive again', so that the feelings supporting the relationship are given current power. The person recalled can be present physically or be located elsewhere. In the first case the physical presence in itself will evoke memories of selected data and feelings. In the second case, where there is no physical presence, the mind can recreate the

---

[1] Jim Cotter (1996), *Love Re-membered – Resources for a House Eucharist*, p. 38.

[2] Applying this process to the Eucharist, Martin Stringer comments: 'What we can see here is a process very similar to that described by Frederick Barth for the Baktaman of New Guinea (1975). Certain key "symbols" are transformed by continual association and disassociation with others to generate a constantly shifting field of "meaning" . . . At this level the mass, any mass, becomes real "anamnesis", a "recalling" as much of the detail and associations of an individual's own life as of the life, death and resurrection of Jesus' (Martin D. Stringer (1999), *On the Perception of Worship*, p. 120).

'image' of the person which, with the remembered sayings and events, will recall the feelings involved in the relationship. Whether such a person is present or absent physically, memories will affect the way we relate to another person. Where the memories are hurtful, effort will need to be made to supersede them or overlay them with affirming memories.[3]

Remembering Jesus

When we apply these general observations to the accounts we have of the early Church we can follow the process by which the disciples must have remembered Jesus. As people who had spent much time in a group, they would gather together and many of these gatherings would be occasions for sharing a meal. At the meal they would recall the key events, the vital sayings and the feelings that they had shared with Jesus and with one another in the group. In particular the memory would be stimulated by the meal and the remembered meals that they had shared with Jesus. As Eugene La Verdiere has written:

> According to this historical reconstruction, at the very beginning, in their celebration of the Eucharist, the early Christians spoke of Jesus' appearance and presence with them. Very soon, they also told stories of Jesus' passion and resurrection. Only later did they concentrate on the Last Supper and what Jesus did and said on 'the night he was handed over'.[4]

Reinterpretation of the Data

The experiences of the Risen Christ caused the disciples to re-evaluate their memories of Jesus – that is the data concerning his actions, words and relationships both before and at the time of his death; and also of their feelings of shame and confusion that his death and their reaction to it had caused. The new data about resurrection helped the disciples reinterpret their memories, and create new memories.[5] Luke 24:13–35 is a key passage which shows how the disciples reinterpreted some of their memories. Luke illustrates how the walk to Emmaus was a journey of transformation which in itself created a powerful new memory that forged links with the experience of new disciples. I note eight steps in the process:

---

[3] See further consideration in Chapter 7.

[4] La Verdiere, Eugene (1996), *The Eucharist in the New Testament and the Early Church*, p. 14. I found this book an excellent guide to the interpretation of key passages in the New Testament.

[5] Oscar Cullman comments: 'Thus the Lord's presence was re-experienced during these love-feasts, both as a recollection of the *historical* fact of the Resurrection and as an experience of the *contemporary* fact of his invisible coming in the gathering of Christians assembled "to break bread"; (and as an) *eschatological* fact (in that) He will appear soon for the Messianic Banquet' (O. Cullman and Leenhardt, F.J. (1958), *Essays on the Lord's Supper*).

1   In verse 14 the picture shows how the two disciples talked with one another to share their memories and their feelings. Memories are often brought to the surface by mutual conversation. The dialogue can affirm or realign the memory of data, and can correct the associated feelings to make them realistic to the data.

2   In verse 15 Jesus becomes present during the sharing of memories about him even though he is not seen to be physically present: 'but their eyes were kept from recognizing him'.

3   In verse 18 the 'stranger' evokes the recall of memories and a restatement of the significance of those memories. Telling another person who has no 'memory' of the one remembered or the associated data can force a rememberer to take stock of their own feelings as they rehearse the story. Such a telling can refocus or reinterpret the relationship which the story reveals. Luke spreads the retelling over five verses (verses 19–24). In these verses the data about Jesus' death is set alongside the data about his possible resurrection. They show how the memory of his death is associated with feelings of dashed hopes, and the memory of his possible resurrection with feelings of 'other people's unlikely stories' – especially the fanciful stories told by women.

4   In verse 25 the 'contra' voice is heard, and reinterpretation arises from such a voice. The minds of the disciples take into account another possible explanation of the remembered data. Who originates the 'contra' voice is a mystery only revealed through faith, although many people can attest to the experience of hearing another voice in the processes of the mind. In this case Luke states that the reinterpretation is caused by two factors: the direct voice of the unrecognized Jesus, and the passages of Scripture recalled. The voice heard may also be the remembered voice of Jesus. Luke records that Jesus had earlier spoken of the necessity of his death and the promise of his resurrection.[6]

5   In verse 29 the reinterpretation of the memories gives rise to new feelings of longing and hope. 'Stay with us' is a request to revive the relationship. The two disciples want to retain the opportunity to develop the relationship with this person who understands them but is not yet seen as the embodiment of the memory of Jesus. So far it is only the voice of the counter-interpretation of key events in their memory.

6   Verse 31 sees the memories finally linked together. At the usual supper meal the actions of taking, blessing, breaking and distributing bread connect all the memories to the person of Jesus. The familiarity of the actions triggers the memory. The minds of the two disciples come to that conclusion. The data in their memory links those actions with the remembered actions of Jesus. So the memory 'recognizes' him.

7   In verse 32 the interpretation of the data creates in the disciples new feelings about the relationship: 'Were not our hearts burning within us?' Such feelings

---

6   See Luke 9:21, 18:31 and 24:6.

are connected both to the breaking of the bread and to the reinterpretation of Scripture.

8 In verses 34 and 35 the journey concludes with reaffirmation as the two disciples share their experience with the wider group of disciples, and in turn hear similar experiences of the Risen Christ. The knowledge that others have had similar experiences gives the story an objectivity which it would not otherwise have.

This account of the experiences of two of the extended group of disciples lays down the template of the pattern by which the memories of Jesus were able to come alive within the early Christian community.

Reconnection

It is clear from the New Testament record that some powerful events and experiences relating to the Risen Christ caused the first disciples to interpret afresh their memories and feelings about Jesus. This led to a process of reconnection in their relationship with Jesus. Instead of shutting out their memories of his death as too painful, they took into account their new memories of the appearance of the Risen Lord and felt 'in touch' with him. This reconnection allowed them to reclaim their feelings of love and commitment to Jesus and to the purpose of his coming which he had shared with them. The memories of the past could now be recaptured and enhanced for the present and provide energy for their actions in the future. This process helps us to understand the key word in this study, the word 'to remember'. Professor Stookey has written:

> The same Hebrew understanding of remembrance that allows us to experience anew the past also allows us to experience already the future ... One experiences the past by doing now what was done then; by doing now what will be done later, we already experience the future in our midst.[7]

Around the 'Dinner Table'

We can imagine how the first disciples met around the table at the meal at the end of the working day. This would be the natural place to share the events of the day, and the memories of other days and occasions. If Luke/Acts has some historical basis, which Luke himself claims in the prologue to the Gospel and the introductory passage to the book of the Acts of the Apostles,[8] then the frequent references[9] to

---

[7] L.H. Stookey (1993), *Eucharist – Christ's feast with the Church*, p. 31.

[8] Luke 1:3 and Acts 1:1–2.

[9] See Luke Ch.14 for a cluster of sayings about the evening meal: vv.1–6 Healing at a meal; vv.7–14 A parable about humility and hospitality; vv.15–24 Parable of the Great Feast. See also the Last Supper reference in Luke 22:20; and the Resurrection meals indicated in Luke 24:30 and 41. Acts 1:4 refers to 'eating together', and the 'breaking of the bread' is included in the summary of key activities of the first disciples (Acts 2:42).

meals and bread in Luke/Acts point to the fact that the time of eating was a key occasion on which the disciples found themselves sharing memories of Jesus.

At the meal table we can imagine the conversation: 'Peter, you remember when . . .'; 'John, you remember your reply when . . .'; and 'Mary, how did you feel when . . .?' The sharing of memories would have allowed two things to take place. First the recalling of the incident would refresh the memory of the events/ words and the significance of that for the relationship between the disciples and Jesus. Secondly the recalling of the incident would allow for the group to correct and reinterpret the memories. Gaps in the memory of the individual could be filled in by the group's memory, and other members of the group could reinterpret the meaning of the action or the saying to shed light on its significance, not only for the past but also for the present situation.

The memory of Jesus would also recall the text and the meaning of key passages of Scripture (for us the Old Testament) known to the disciples. Jesus used passages of Scripture to illuminate the significance and meaning of key events in his life. The early Church may well have connected the memory of sayings and events of Jesus with other passages of Scripture to bring together in their minds the voice of God in both the Prophets and the words of Jesus.[10] Because the disciples believed that 'God spake through the prophets', so the memory of their words connected the hearer to Godself. Once the disciples were convinced that Jesus was the Christ[11] they would remember Christ's words as also being the voice of God. In the process of memory the words are connected to the speaker and thus evoke feelings of relationship with the person and not just the message. To remember Jesus' words was to remember Jesus and the relationship between Jesus and the disciple.

At the table the memories of key sayings and events brought back the 'presence' of Jesus and so his teaching could be applied to current problems and policies. All this took place in the context of a meal. The meal itself would bring back memories of the meals that the disciples had shared with Jesus during his earthly life and as part of the resurrection appearances. From the records in the New Testament two meals in particular seem to have been the focus of the disciples' memory. The first was the feeding of a vast crowd of followers in Galilee during the Jesus' time of 'popular' ministry. The second was the Supper that Jesus shared with his inner circle of disciples on the night before his death. Let us examine each in turn.

The Feeding of the Thousands

The feeding of a crowd of thousands is recorded in some form in all four Gospels. In Matthew it is shown in two forms; one the feeding of five thousand where the crowd is from Jewish areas,[12] and the other the feeding of four thousand from the

---

[10] There are a number of examples in Matthew's Gospel of which Matt. 4:14–16 is one.
[11] See Heb. 1:1–2: 'Long ago God spoke to our ancestors in many and various ways by the prophets, but in these last days he has spoken to us by a Son, whom he appointed heir of all things, through whom he also created the worlds.'
[12] Matt. 14:13–21.

Gentile areas on the far side of the Sea of Galilee.[13] In Mark the reference is again to a crowd of followers 'in a deserted place' and the disciples are told by Jesus 'to give them something to eat'.[14] Luke's Gospel locates the scene at Bethsaida (around the lake from Capernaum) and it follows the return of the apostles from their mission. Again the apostles are the ones to distribute the food that Jesus has blessed.[15] John also includes the account and connects the meal with the Passover.[16] Here the story is the prelude to passages in which Jesus declares: 'I am the bread of life. Whoever comes to me will never be hungry, and whoever believes in me will never be thirsty.'[17] The bread of life is shown to be the bread of eternal life in verse 51, and further explained as 'my flesh that I will give for the life of the world'. So in John's Gospel the crowd is fed with Christ as the Passover sacrifice. Here we can trace how memories of feeding a crowd were linked with memories of Jesus and his sayings, and also linked with other memories of the Passover sacrifice. In tabular form the sequence is:

A.	The sharing of food	>>>	memory of
B.	Jesus sharing food	>>>	memory of
C.	Jesus feeding a crowd	>>>	memory of
D.	Jesus giving life to the world	>>>	memory of
E.	Jesus as the Passover sacrifice.		

The Last Supper in the Gospel Record

The second major meal event which predominated in the memory of the first disciples was the Supper Jesus shared with the inner group of disciples on the night prior to his death. This Supper is recorded in some form in all four gospels.

Matthew clearly says that this is a Passover meal.[18] The Supper itself begins with the betrayal scene and this is followed by the words that Jesus said over the bread and the cup. The conclusion has a reference to the future: 'that day when I drink it new in my Father's kingdom'.[19] The memory of the Passover is brought out in the words: 'this is my blood of the covenant poured out for many for the forgiveness of sins'.

Matthew's version is based closely on the account found in Mark which has the same features of Passover, institution and the future day of the kingdom.[20]

In the Luke version[21] the reference to the Passover in chapter 22 is even more pronounced: 'I have eagerly desired to eat this Passover with you before I suffer' (v.15), and the future stressed in the repetition of the words: 'I will not eat it until

---

[13] Matt. 15:32–39.
[14] Mark 6:37.
[15] Luke 9:10–17.
[16] John 6:1–14; see v.4 'Now the Passover, the festival of the Jews, was near.'
[17] John 6:35.
[18] Matt. 26:19.
[19] Matt. 26:20–25 for the betrayal; vv. 26–28 for the words with the bread and cup.
[20] Mark 14:12–25.
[21] Luke 22:9–23.

it is fulfilled in the kingdom of God', and 'I will not drink of the fruit of the vine until the kingdom of God comes' (v.15 and v.18). Luke is the only gospel writer who records the words: 'Do this in remembrance of me' (v.19). It is said over the loaf, but not in association with the cup. In Luke the betrayal reference comes after the blessing of the cup.

In John's Gospel the Last Supper is the occasion for the last discourses and the accounts stretch for chapters rather than verses.[22] The occasion is a 'Supper' which takes place *before* the Festival of the Passover.[23] The account begins with the knowledge of Judas' betrayal and continues with the washing of the disciples' feet and teaching about its meaning. The betrayal is a sub-theme to all this section and the sharing of the bread between the betrayer and the betrayed is poignantly recorded. The need for mutual love within the context of betrayal and denial (illustrated by the warning to Peter) is part of the teaching in this section at the end of chapter 13. Chapter 14 begins the discourse proper in which Jesus describes himself as the way to the Father (vv.1–14) and promises the Father's gift of the Spirit to give comfort to the disciples and inspire them with love. It is this Spirit which will 'remind you of all that I have said to you' (v.26). John, out of the experience of the later Church, tells how the Spirit will prompt the disciples' memory and help to create the presence of Jesus for them. The reference to the cup provides the opportunity for a long discourse (John 15–16:33) on the symbol of the vine, and thereby the unity, love, joy and peace amidst persecution that is Jesus' gift to the community. In chapter 17 the discourse becomes Jesus' prayer for the disciples' faithfulness and protection, and this prayer returns to the theme of mutual love, first between the Father and the Son, and then between the Son and the disciples. So the love of Christ becomes incarnate in his new body, that is, the disciples. It should be noted that in John's Gospel there are no actual words of 'institution' relating to the bread and the cup.

This survey of the record in the Gospels of the last meal that Jesus shared with his disciples shows that the event is always stated as a meal, but the words and meaning are given various interpretations in each different gospel.

The Lord's Supper in the Epistles

Alongside these records from the four Gospels we must place Paul's letter to the Corinthian Church which scholars believe is probably the earlier written record. This letter by Paul obviously responds to certain questions raised by that Church community about some practical difficulties in maintaining harmony. The root cause of the disunity is the lack of love and respect between members.[24] For Paul a proper understanding of, and participation in, the Lord's Supper is the key to the resolution of the issues. As Eugene La Verdiere says:

---

[22] John Chapters 13–17.
[23] John 13:1–2.
[24] 1 Cor. 11:18.

At Corinth, the words and gestures had become empty because the Corinthian community no longer did what Jesus did. Their Eucharist was no longer a remembrance of Christ's passion and resurrection, no longer expressed what he did 'on the night he was handed over'. As such the community was no longer acting as a link in the chain of Eucharistic tradition, handing on to others what had been handed on to them. That is why Paul told them their supper was no longer 'the Lord's Supper'.[25]

The tradition, the memory, that Paul had received 'from the Lord' he handed on to the Corinthians.[26] This same tradition has influenced the wording in all the liturgies that have been drawn up to assist the Church in every generation celebrate the Lord's Supper – a name that Paul used in this letter. In Paul's tradition the threefold action of taking, blessing and breaking the bread is accompanied by the words:

> This is my body that is for you (or in some texts 'is broken for you').
> Do this in remembrance of me. (v.24)

The taking of the cup (clearly a cup of wine) is accompanied by the words:

> This cup is the new covenant in my blood.
> Do this, as often as you drink it,
> in remembrance of me. (v.25)

Here the Last Supper connects the meal to the person of the host, Jesus, and because of his words it is also connected to the action of Christ in offering himself as a Passover sacrifice through his death on the Cross. The sacrifice keeps in our memory the covenant with God on which we rely for our relationship with God and with one another as the body of Christ.

Development of Memory

As we have traced these New Testament references to a meal remembered by the early disciples it is possible to observe the increasing circles of memory which their shared meals must have generated:

- The meal was the *occasion* when the disciples shared their vivid first-hand memories of who Jesus was, what he did, and what he said.
- The meal was the *means* by which the memories 'refreshed/re-presented' the presence of Jesus as the one who used to be at table with the disciples and is now present again through memory.
- The meal was the *sign* of the presence of Christ as the bread embodied the person and the wine embodied the sacrifice which restored (like the Passover Lamb) the relationship between God and the worshipper.
- The meal so connected the disciples to Christ that the bread was *in reality*

---

[25] La Verdiere (1996), p. 42.
[26] 1 Cor. 11:23–26.

his body, and the cup of wine was his blood – both given and shared for the salvation of all.

In this way the Last Supper (something to be treasured as a memory of Jesus before his death) became the Lord's Supper[27] (something which recreated in the mind the true presence of Christ as the Lord to whom the disciple is now fully committed). This Lord's Supper was the experience of life in the kingdom where God and all created beings lived in unity of purpose and harmony of relationship. It was the true 'shalom' and as such satisfied the mind and all the emotions in their quest to bring together all things in their proper place.

The Meal, the Passion and the Passover

The connection between the meal and the passion of Christ, and between the meal, his death and the Passover seems to have been very influential in the developmental process. Because of the linkages that the memory can make, one event and occasion can take on the meaning and significance of the other.

For the disciples the meals they shared linked them to the Last Supper and to the occasion of its celebration at Passover time. John's Gospel even goes so far as to link the time of the death of Jesus on the cross with the time of the sacrifice of the Passover lambs.[28] In this tradition Jesus is the Lamb of God offered for the sake of the world. Memory now has found significance in the purpose of Christ's death. The brain can harmonize the connections because it has given greatest weight to the significance of the event. This significance places importance on the relationship created through Christ's death, and shows this through amending the timing of the occasion. The death is not significant in itself but as the opportunity for a new relationship between the worshipper and God. This equates with the relationship established at the Passover. The meal is therefore the means by which I appropriate for myself as a disciple the work of Christ for the salvation of the whole world.

The Meal and the Resurrection

The common factor of a meal allows the memory to make a further linkage. The significance of the Passion is linked to the significance of the resurrection by the celebration of a community meal. The record in Acts and Corinthians[29] indicates that at the weekly remembrance the first disciples celebrated the meal as a commemoration *of the resurrection* 'with glad and generous hearts'.[30] The first day of the week became a signal for the memory to link the meal with the resurrection

---

[27] 1 Cor. 11:20.
[28] John 19:31.
[29] Acts 20:7 and 1 Cor. 16:2.
[30] Acts 2:46.

event and as we have seen this observation is confirmed by the timing of the resurrection appearances in Luke 24:1 and 24:13. It is further confirmed by the appearance of Jesus at the meal in the house of the two disciples at Emmaus.

In much later years confusion arose when the remembrance in the meal became too attached to the death of Christ and there was a failure to keep in mind the New Testament link with the resurrection. From what we have learnt about the ways memory can operate, both the death and the resurrection can be held together as giving full meaning to the meal. One event is necessary for the interpretation of the other. The death of Christ would be seen as a sacrifice only when it was recognized that God had received the sacrifice and showed 'approval' by raising Jesus from the dead. The meal helps us to appreciate that the death was not an end but a new beginning, empowering us through forgiveness of sin to live the risen life.

In Remembrance of Me

The phrase that Paul uses in 1 Corinthians and which Luke repeats for the bread needs further examination.

Does it simply mean that we are to use the bread (and wine) as a way of remembering Jesus, as a stimulus to our memory of him? The answer is probably 'no', but the wording cannot mean any *less* than this. As we have discovered, our memory allows us to link data, with significance, with relationship. The data in this case is that Jesus shared a meal with the first disciples and made clear that, through the bread, the disciples would be able to be in touch with him even when his physical body was no longer visible.[31] As a photograph stimulates the memory of a person so the bread (meal) would stimulate the memory of Jesus Christ. But the memory was not simply of a person. It was also of what that person had done in relationship to us. The memory was also of the work of Jesus – his passion and resurrection – and by it the forgiveness of sin and the new life which we could receive. The bread was linked to Christ, broken for us on the cross and now our Risen Lord; and the wine was linked to Christ, the cup of suffering that brought joy to the world. So through the bread and wine our memories are able to relate to Jesus and what he has done for us and all the people of the world.

The word *to remember* is linked by its usage in Hebrew to a further development of this concept. In Hebrew *zakar* (to remember or cause to remember) is linked by passages in Genesis to the memory that God has for the covenant that God has made with humanity. In Genesis 9:15 the rainbow reminds God of the covenant between God and all creatures so that the flood shall never again be a cause of total destruction. So God can say 'I will remember my covenant.' The rainbow is

---

[31] The traditional view of this memory was expressed by Thomas Merton: 'When we go to the altar to receive the Host from the hands of the priest, we are mystically present at the Holy Supper in which with His own hands Jesus broke bread, which has been changed into His Sacred Body, and distributed it to His Apostles,' from Thomas Merton (1956), *The Living Bread* (reprinted 1983), p. 34.

the cause by which God remembers the relationship re-established with humanity. Likewise Jesus' death is a cause for God to remember the new covenant by which we are offered forgiveness of sin. What Jesus did is a cause for both God and humanity to remember the relationship which is built on total love and full forgiveness that leads to restoration of life.

This link with the word *zakar* has led to an understanding of the words of Christ as recorded in Paul's tradition to mean 'Do this as my memorial, my sacrifice, which causes God to remember this new covenant.'[32]

A 'Real' Presence

It is Luke's Gospel which links the idea of remembrance to the bread. The bread is the means whereby we can link the memory with the person. Through the bread we form a link in the mind with the Jesus known to us from the data and the feelings which we experience in our relationship with him. Memory can easily recreate for us all that makes the person 'real' for us. Through memory the person comes alive for us again. We hear the voice; we see the face; we feel the touch; we are moved by the words; we are empowered by the inspiration of whatever makes the relationship significant for us.

It is in this way that people say they can remember a person who is significant for them. The memory may be of past events and feelings that were once 'in the flesh', but memory can also make those events and feelings alive for the present 'in the spirit'. By the expression 'in the flesh' we are referring to a physical time and place. By the expression 'in the spirit' we are indicating factors which release events and feelings from a particular time and place and making them independent of the physical. Such events and feelings have lasting significance and are powerful long after the time and place span in which they occurred. Memory is the faculty that allows this to happen. Memory makes something or someone present for us in an instant, once our brains can make the connections. Our memory differentiates between the past and the immediate present, but the reality of something or someone is not dependent on the time/place factor. The brain would be said to be not functioning if the memory has no idea whether the event/feeling is new or old. Normally the memory has the capacity to keep past things current in their significance and meaning for us. As we shall see in Chapter 10 memory can also help the brain create pictures of what might be in the future. So it is right to claim that memory holds the past and the future together in the present.

---

[32] Louis Bouyer comments: 'This word must be given the sense that it always has in the rabbinical literature and especially the liturgical literature of the period. It in no way means a subjective, human psychological act of returning to the past, but an objective reality destined to make something or some one perpetually present before God and for God himself. As Max Thurian so well showed, this notion of "memorial" is not only an essential ritual element of certain sacrifices, but one that gives ultimate significance to every sacrifice, and eminently to the Passover sacrifice' from Louis Bouyer (1968), *Eucharist: Theology and Spirituality of the Eucharistic Prayer*, p. 103–4.

There have been many arguments down the generations about the ways that Christ is present in the Liturgy of the Eucharist.[33] Sadly many of these arguments forgot to look at the way the human brain works and began to use philosophy or other scientific examples to find ways to describe the means of Christ's presence. The argument as to whether a sign or symbol could be said 'to be' what it signified or symbolized overlooked the fact that the mind could distinguish between the difference without being tied to an either/or position. In one sense the mind knows that a sign is still a sign. However with another sense the mind knows that the sign can allow us to relate to what is signified. The bread of the Eucharist is of course bread. I have no doubt that this is what Jesus intended so that we could link the basic substance of food with God the creator and the giver of all things. *And* I also have no doubt that Jesus knew that the bread would be able to convey his presence and purpose to all his disciples. Because he had related bread to his body and wine to the blood of his sacrifice, his disciples could remember his full self and what he had done for humanity. The image in our memory is no less real than the image in the brain that the eye sends from the data received on the first occasion.

Memory and Faith

What then is the connection between memory and faith? Can faith so fool memory that the mind believes what cannot be true because faith somehow creates false impressions?[34] Faith seems to be the judgment/decision-making faculty in the brain which advises memory whether such an event or feeling is appropriate for the situation. In this sense all people exercise faith constantly. We make assumptions that certain things are appropriate. For example I trust the stairs to hold me up whenever I climb to the next level. Memory recalls the previous experiences of moving up the stairs and not falling down. Faith judges that this memory is appropriate for the current situation.

Religious faith works in the same way. We test the data, the feelings and the experiences in a relationship with God, and faith affirms that what the memory recalls is still appropriate for the ongoing situation. If we discover a sense of the

---

[33] David Cairns sums this debate: 'When the Sacrament was celebrated, men were not merely remembering an event in the dim and receding past. Christ was really and truly there . . . But in spite of these debates [as to how Jesus was present] it is today true, as it has been all along, that the great majority of Christian people are united in the belief that Christ is truly present in the Lord's Supper, and that in it, in a mysterious communion, he gives himself and his benefits to those who receive him in humble faith', from David Cairns (1967), *In Remembrance of Me – Aspects of the Lord's Supper*, p. 34.

[34] David Cairns argues that if we say that Christ is present by faith, the faith of the recipient, then we must be careful not to press the point out of perspective. Christ will not be *more* present because some are *more* full of faith. Rather faith is the means by which we perceive the presence of Christ in the Sacrament. See pp. 36–8 in Cairns (1967). Cairns quotes Dr Donald Baillie, *Theology of the Sacraments* (London 1957), p. 99: 'Faith is the channel by which God's most intimate presence comes to men in this earthly life.'

presence and power of Christ in the Eucharist, then memory accumulates these experiences and recalls them as requested. Faith then judges whether the recalled experiences are still appropriate to our situation. Faith cannot create the experiences but it can judge their appropriateness for us, but not for others. Faith can be shared, and as human beings we need to share faith with one another or we will be exhausted judging everything *de novo* for ourselves. Yet even shared faith has to be accepted through faith by each person.

Thus it is right to say that Jesus is present to the faithful. Jesus can also be present to those seeking an experience of him if they are open to that possibility. The way the faithful maintain their memories of the data, feelings and experiences in their relationship with Jesus profoundly affects those who seek faith to exercise it.

Remembering Christ through the Eucharist

Liturgy is one of the prime means by which disciples learn to remember Christ and discover the faith which determines the importance and application of this relationship for their lives. As we look at each section of the Liturgy in turn, we can see that in every part there are ways for a disciple to remember Christ.

Prayer and Praise   The beginning of the liturgy opens up the minds of the worshippers to the sense of the relationship which exists between each worshipper and God. Unless it is made clear that this relationship is possible, the worshippers will find no significance in the 'memory' of events shared with the worshippers during the liturgy. In the first acts of prayer and praise the worshippers 'remember' their relationship with God and acknowledge God's memory for them as disciples of Christ.

Repentance and Forgiveness   In this section of the liturgy the worshippers remember the work of Christ on the Cross which gives them encouragement to turn back to Christ, confess their sins and hear again the declaration of the forgiveness of God. This section causes the faithful to remember Christ's work of salvation – his words and actions to declare sinners forgiven, and his sacrifice on the cross for the salvation of the world.

The Ministry of the Word   The readings from Scripture and especially from the Gospels link the memory of the worshippers with the works and words of Christ. In the sermon the Word of God is broken and shared so that it touches the lives of the worshippers. The 'memory' is of Christ speaking and acting two thousand years ago, and also of Christ's living word being applied to situations over many generations including our own. The individual memory of the worshipper is able to hold together the memory of the data and the memory of its application in a variety of corporate and individual situations. This allows Christ to be 'present' to the situation of the moment. The way that the Scripture and the sermon is presented will help (or hinder) the worshipper's use of their memory faculty for this purpose.

The Creed   The Creed is the summary of the memory and the faith of the corporate Church. The recitation of the Creed helps the worshippers remember who God is and what God has done. It also helps them remember who they are and what together they believe as the Church. The Creed keeps the worshippers in memory of the relationship they have with God and with one another as the Christian community.

The Prayers of Intercession   The prayers help the worshippers remember the Ascended Christ as the one who constantly upholds the world in prayer that it might fulfill the purposes of God.[35] The Intercessions in the liturgy remind the worshippers that they are called to join Christ in their prayers as part of his body on earth. The prayers of Intercession will also inspire actions of care for those in need in the community.

The Peace   The sharing of the Peace activates the memory of Christ for the worshippers in two ways. First it helps them recall the words of the Risen Christ to the first disciples after the resurrection: 'Peace be with you.'[36] Through the memory of these words worshippers will have experienced the peace of Christ in the midst of the storms of life. Their minds will recall these feelings and affirm the peace shared by Christ in the liturgy. Secondly the sharing of the peace between members of the body of Christ activates memories of mutual love and support which makes physical the words in the Peace. For a small number of worshippers memories of hurtful physical touch will make them shrink back from sharing the Peace with others in this way. Such memories need to be healed through good pastoral care, as outlined in Chapter 7.

The Great Thanksgiving Prayer   The act of thanksgiving prompts our memories to recall the reasons why thanksgiving should be offered. In this prayer the worshippers, as in the Creed, are reminded of what God has done for them and therefore their faith in the goodness of God is rekindled. Christ becomes the focus in this prayer as it recalls his passion, resurrection and ascension and the words he spoke on the night before he died. This *anamnesis* (the remembrance/memorial) in the words of Institution helps worshippers to remember vividly Christ and all his work. Because the words 'Remember me' are repeated twice the worshippers are most conscious at this point in the liturgy of the way that their memory focuses Christ's presence. My thesis in this chapter is that the worshippers will reap most benefit from this remembrance if they are helped to see the breadth of activity that 'memory' possesses. To think of remembering only as an action of looking back into the past is too restrictive. Memory can hold together the past, the present and the future at any point in time. Such memory is enfolded in the relationship between the worshipper and Christ so that it forms part of the trust between them both and highlights the significance of this relationship.

---

[35]   See my book *Ascension Now – Implications of Christ's Ascension for Today's Church* (2001), especially Ch. 6.
[36]   Luke 24:36.

This prayer also acknowledges the activity of the Spirit as the inspirer of memory[37] and as the agent of the full Godhead in this present act of worship. In his last address Max Thurian declared:

> The Holy Spirit makes the crucified and risen Christ really present for us in the eucharistic meal by fulfilling the promise contained in the words of institution of the Lord's Supper. The role of the Holy Spirit in the eucharist is to make the historical words of Christ real and alive.[38]

The Spirit is not only active in maintaining the connection between the bread and the wine, and the body of Christ but also in holding the connection between the body of Christ and the community of the Church. Through the activity of the Spirit both are experienced as 'the body of Christ', that is, ways in which Christ is present and active for the worshippers.

Distribution of the Sacrament   In the breaking of the bread the worshippers remember the Passion of Christ and the work of salvation. The worshippers in receiving the bread and the wine appropriate the memory of Christ and salvation to themselves, and in memory and in physical touch re-experience their incorporation into Christ so that they become what they receive.

Affirmation of the Body and its Work   The final section of the liturgy is an affirmation by the community that it is indeed the body of Christ and is dedicated to the work of the body in mission and care for the world. This part of the liturgy is a call to remember who we are and what we are called to be and do. It may include a prayer of oblation, a blessing and a dismissal. All these prayers should establish a memory with which to leave the place of worship so that the worshippers are carried forward into their life situations assured of Christ's presence and committed to Christ's work.

Summary   The whole of the Liturgy of the Eucharist is an occasion and a means by which the worshippers can remember Christ, and in their faith apply that memory to their relationship with Christ. They will remember that they have become the body of Christ – the community of the Church – and that they are called to a life of witness and service in the world. There their memory of Christ's presence and power will enable their ministry.

---

[37]   Professor Stookey writes: 'Before going to the cross, Jesus tells the disciples, "The Holy Spirit . . . will teach you everything, and remind you of all that I have said to you" (John 14:26). This functioning of "reminding" is closely akin to anamnesis and has sometimes given the Spirit the title of "The Remembrancer". Hence, what we specially "do in remembrance" of Jesus is done through the agency of the Holy Spirit', L.H. Stookey (1993), *Eucharist*, p. 100.

[38]   Max Thurian (1998), 'The Lima Liturgy', p. 18.

Chapter 6

Corporate Memory

The Group and the Individual

In my two introductory chapters on how the brain and the memory function operate, I outlined the way that individuals 'learnt' from those around them. I showed in Chapter One[1] how we literally have to learn from others how to think. In Chapter 2 I recorded how the brain is wired to imitate and lays down memories to be applied in future action.[2] Individuals need a supporting group to accumulate experiences which provide the memories on which they base their learning as to how to act.

Each person learns by watching, listening, modeling, revising and re-trying. This process lays down a 'highway' in the brain which speeds up the possibility of repeating the actions on future occasions. Each individual learns from the group's experience and retained memory, and continues to react with the group for further learning and implementation to take place. Accustomed to the process, we take for granted the interdependence between ourselves and others. Modern society has glorified the individual to such an extent that the role of the group is hardly mentioned. However from what we have learnt about the brain and the memory function we cannot ignore the influence of the group on the behaviour and ability of the individual.

The individual borrows from the group's memory in four ways:

- *Through natural sharing, observation and modeling* – The corporate memory influences the individual through a progressive circle of people. The inner group is the most powerful in its influence. These are the people with whom we live most closely – our family, however that is defined in our complex world. Beyond the inner core is a circle of an extended family from which the intimate family has absorbed many of its principles and traditions, retained in its memory. Beyond that again is a wider society which has set down the regulations for living in a diverse community. This may be a regional or state system of government. Across the boundaries of nations there is a corporate identity which influences the individual through the reports and opinions carried by the news media. The Internet has strengthened for many this circle of memory. The individual, however independent, observes what others are doing and how they are acting, and reacts with and to this corporate memory.

---

[1] See the paragraph on 'Thinking' on page 2.
[2] See the paragraph 'Wired to imitate' on page 12.

- *Through formal teaching* – Each group in these circles sees itself as responsible for the instruction of its members. At first the teaching is the prime responsibility of the inner family; then the wider family group passes on its wisdom and experience, giving instruction on its family's history, standards and key experiences. The local society also believes that it has a duty to provide formal schooling to share not only information but also common standards and principles. The international community in turn believes that it has a duty to share its knowledge with each new generation through print and electronic media. Such teaching is the result of research and the sharing of life experiences. At every level each group gives formal teaching to its new young members.

- *Through the sharing of rituals that are associated with the life of the group* – Each of the circles of community has key rituals to pass on to the individual a sense of identity and belonging. Who I am is to know to whom I belong and where I can stand with security. The various rituals mark membership and an ownership of a place to call home. Many races consider the connection to family, clan and land as essential for the health of the individual. To reinforce this sense of belonging they have developed elaborate rituals which are regularly repeated to ensure that both the individual and the group retain the memory of their essential connections.

- *Through hearing and repeating the corporate 'songs and sayings' of the various communities* – Each new generation is helped, by participation rather than by formal instruction, to learn the group's own songs and wisdom sayings. Song is an especially powerful means of stating and restating a group's identity. There are family favourites; there are school songs and mottoes; there are national anthems – all of which form part of the deep memory of each member of the group. To sing such a song or to repeat such a saying not only keeps its memory fresh but also refreshes the sense of belonging to the group and its corporate identity. We note this when on great sporting occasions the song of the team or the song of the nation is the means by which we feel and identify with those who share our community. Through these songs, recalled from our memory, we know who we are and to whom we belong.[3]

In all these four ways the individual and the group interact and lay down memories that intertwine so that each forms and feels part of the other and its memories.

---

[3] See Pfatteicher, Philip H. (1995), *The School of the Church – Worship and Christian Formation*, p. 68: 'The place to which music and song admit us, Zuckerkandl insists, is a place of unity, of communion with self with all else that is. Song annihilates distance and time, joining present experience with past experiences. Past and present are experienced simultaneously.'

The Corporate and the Individual in Liturgy

It is not difficult to see the application of the above to the work of liturgy in the corporate community of the Church. The liturgy utilizes these four means of sharing the group's memory with each individual member. By participation in the liturgy each person is able to absorb naturally the corporate experience of the presence and power of God. In liturgy, formal teaching is given in the Bible readings and in the sermon. In liturgy, ritual passes on the experience of membership and identity, particularly in the sacraments of Baptism and Eucharist. In liturgy, songs and sayings link us with one another and with the past so that we know that we are all God's people.

It is the liturgy of the Church which formulates and keeps alive the corporate memory of being Church. The elements by which this corporate memory is built up are:

- *Telling of the 'story' of Christ's life, death, resurrection and ascension* – The memories of the story of Christ are interwoven with the memories of the stories that Christ himself told. Then the story of Christ continues with the story of how each new generation has made that story their story as they encounter Christ in their day and place. Scripture, story and encounter are bound together to form our corporate memory of Christ.

- *Sharing in the corporate rituals* – The rituals of the Church give sense form to this story. The story of Christ's baptism, and of the disciples' baptism, is embedded in the ritual of baptism for the newest disciple. The story of Christ healing the sick, and of the healing of the sick through the prayers of the Church down the ages, is given sense form in the ritual of praying with and anointing those who are sick now. The story of the Last Supper, and of the breaking of the bread with the Risen Christ, is ritualized in the sacrament of Holy Communion celebrated for this community.

- *Teaching about the nature of God and the faith of the Church* – The corporate memory of the Church is expressed in the repetition of the Creeds during worship. The memory of the Creed is enhanced whenever it is given corporate expression in chant or song by all the members of the worshipping community. In more recent history hymns and songs which express Christian faith have powerfully influenced the corporate memory of who God is and how God acts.

Repetition for Retention

The corporate memory can only be retained when the memories in all these various forms are repeated by the group on a regular basis. In Chapter 2 we took note of how this repetition is a requirement for the individual because of the way the brain and the memory function. What is true for the individual is true also for the group.

Repetition in itself is not sufficient to retain memories because the brain constantly accumulates further data and experiences, and must release memory space. Retention requires both repetition and a weighting of significance. For significance to occur in a corporate situation repetition has to be accompanied by a sense of application and a sense of belonging to the group. Belonging has an emotional content and application has an intellectual and practical content. Both contribute to a sense of the meaningfulness of life. Because of its nature, religion is a powerful stimulus to corporate memory. Religious memory deals with a sense of who I am and what I should do to find life satisfying and fulfilling. Religious communities are able to create strong corporate memories and retain these for each new context encountered.

The corporate memory of a community begins to fade whenever a sense of belonging weakens, when the application of the memory no longer seems appropriate to the new context, when ritual ceases to engender a sense of emotional support, and when the corporate memory is fractured by arguments about how the rituals should be conducted or by divisions about the truth of the statements of faith.

The frequency of the repetition of memories within the group is vital for their retention. The pressures of so many activities in modern society mean that attendance of every member at group meetings is not regular enough to retain a strong sense of corporate memory. Because of the absence of some members not all experience the same 'story', and gradually the memory becomes individualized. The remembered story becomes that of the individual's experience and not that of the group as a whole. In religious terms the retained memory is an experience of God whenever a person finds that, rather than a corporate experience of God as found *within* the meeting of the Church community.

An example of the break-up of the corporate memory can be found in relation to the practice of the sacrament of Baptism. For many years baptism was experienced by the Church community as the ritual which was frequently repeated within the assembly as each new disciple and each child of Christian parents was baptized into Christ and made a member of Christ's Church. However in more recent times in some churches baptism of a child has become the ritual of the family. It represents a celebration of a birth in their family and of God's relationship with their child. Baptism in these circumstances does not reaffirm the corporate memory of the saving work of Christ. Instead the spotlight is on the child and its birth into an individual family. Thus a key factor for the corporate memory – a sense of every member participating and belonging – was lost. Baptism no longer refreshed the memory of my baptism and my responsibility for every baptized disciple and child within my community.

Memory and Context

For corporate memory to be retained, significance as well as repetition is required. Significance implies that the memory can be applied to the life situations of the members of the group. Gordon Lathrop has written:

A community doing its liturgy will be remembering the series of rituals that the participants have known and will be reorganizing, reinterpreting, and reforming – criticizing – those memories by means of ongoing ritual enactment.[4]

This act of reinterpreting is in relation to the new context which is always evolving. The application of the corporate memory requires the memory to be able to fit each new context. Since life evolves rather than remains static, the context of life is both new and connected to the past. As religion is primarily focused on relationships rather than material matters, the context of relationships is more important than material circumstances. That is why the quality of relationships within the group determines the context, and this in turn strengthens or weakens the corporate memory. When the relationships lack depth, or the relationships are broken by conflict, the corporate memory of who the group is and what the group is for is forgotten in the pain of the remembered broken relationships. People leave the group because they do not wish to tolerate these painful memories.

For the corporate memory to be sustained, the past memory of the group must be able to be applied to the present context. Lathrop relates this principle to the ritual of the Eucharist:

The mercy of God comes to liturgical expression as our memories are brought to the crisis of the present juxtaposition: this particular text, done again now, set against this food, pressed again now into our hands, drawing our memories into the current memory and hope of the church.[5]

This Eucharist rebinds us to Christ and the Church as the body of Christ because Christ lives in the corporate memory of the Church, and we live his life in our daily life now. The past becomes present and guides and sustains our future. 'Give us today our daily bread' is the worshipper's cry. We want our memory of Christ to be as fresh as the newly baked loaf from today's oven. We want this new loaf to sustain our daily living. Unless the memory applies to each new context, then the bread will soon be rejected as stale. Eugene La Verdiere, also writing about the Eucharist, makes a similar point: 'The community must be able to meet new challenges and the traditions must be able to develop. For that, traditions needs to be both resilient and open, which is a delicate balance to maintain.'[6]

Memory and Change

The brain constantly applies the recorded data to a changed situation. From the beginning the brain has learnt that very few situations are exactly the same. Learning to walk is a memorized activity but every action of walking is different. The ground is never exactly the same. It varies in height, slope and surface, and

---

[4] Lathrop, Gordon W. (1993), *Holy Things – A Liturgical Theology*, p. 180.
[5] Ibid., p. 127.
[6] La Verdiere, Eugene (1996), *The Eucharist in the New Testament and the Early Church*, p. 130.

there are different wind pressures. So the memory of walking is applied to the changed context of this walk. To climb up steps the brain adjusts new data, recorded by the eye and the feet about this set of steps, to the stored memory. As we move we hardly consider the difficulty unless the steps are so steep as to cause us to be out of breath, or our eyes fail so that we cannot see the step's height and we fall.

Taking this example we can see that the difficulty for the corporate memory in trying to apply it to the changed circumstances arises from *the degree of change* and from *the pace of change*. When these are extreme the corporate memory has difficulty in adapting to the changed context.

For the Church the degree of change will always be apparent when there is a major disruption in relationships. War, migration, natural disaster, economic chaos – all cause a major strain on relationships. For a while people may turn to the corporate memory for support as they face the crisis of change. However if the corporate memory cannot be applied to the radical new circumstances, then the corporate memory will lapse as not being effective any more. In the history of the people of God in the First Testament, the exile of the Israelites from Egypt, and the exile of the people from Jerusalem, were two such 'turning points' in the corporate memory. After disruption the corporate memory was able to reapply the memory to the new context and formulate a new story by which they were bound, as one people, to God through a covenant. Because relationships are vital to corporate identity and to the sense of belonging, renewed relationships are the key to the continuance of the corporate memory in times of dramatic change.

Memory and Identity

Corporate memory is essential to our sense of identity. Among the indigenous peoples of New Zealand the rituals of welcome and response establish the right of the local people to live in this place, and the 'mana' (sense of value and respect) of the visitors. Each speaker stands to proclaim their relationship to the ancestors and the clan, to the mountain, the river and the earth of this location, and to the gathered assembly. The stories about these people and these places are repeated frequently in speech and in song. 'I am' because 'I belong' is the principle of the culture. As an elder it is my duty to learn and pass on these stories and songs because if the corporate memory ceases, I and my clan cease to be. I am nobody unless I know my place in the pattern of relationships to people and the land. As the language is the medium by which these stories and songs are embodied in the corporate memory, so the language becomes a vital part of the community's identity.

There are many parallels between this racial memory and the Christian corporate memory. Our individual sense of identity remains strong when we know how we relate to God and to the Christian community. The corporate memory enfolds us as we take our place as a member of this Church. We learn to speak of our ancestors as our own. They are family, not strangers, even though they are of a different generation, place, race and culture to ours. We tell the story of the Church as our story, our history, our successes and our failures. We learn to relate to this holy place where prayer has hallowed the walls with the presence of God, and where people have found new strength for the journey through life. We relate to this current assembly of Christians as those with whom we are dedicated to undertake God's will, and with whom we share daily bread.

The corporate memory creates a sense of identity and calls forth from its members the duty of repetition and application. The sharing of memories and rituals creates the substance for the continuation of the corporate memory. Each new crisis, each new success, becomes incorporated into the memory by story and song.[7]

Memory and Story

We have noted the importance of story in the maintenance of the corporate memory. In a club or society the stories of the past are a vital part of all social functions. Over the tea cups or the beer glasses the reminiscences weave a story of people and places which provides the fabric that holds that society together. Such stories mark the foundation and the turning points of the corporate memory.

In the same way a national or regional community tells each new generation its story of formation and reformation. These stories are often retold on days of national remembrance: a treaty signed, a war won or lost, a current structure of government decided. These stories are essential to a sense of nationhood and corporate belonging. The story is often supported by rituals: a gathering of national leaders, a remembrance service at the War Memorial, a citizens' parade. Sometimes the outline of the story is told when new citizens are welcomed and given the documents of belonging.

Within the Church the story is rehearsed in the liturgical cycle of the year, and repeated in summary in the sacraments of membership and integration (Baptism and Eucharist). Throughout the year the total narrative is divided into pieces that can be more easily grasped. The annual cycle begins with Christmas, progresses to Holy Week and Easter, and then to Pentecost and the Sundays that follow as 'ordinary time' so that the teaching applied to daily living can be maintained. Interspersed throughout this cycle are the remembrances of the heroes and heroines of the faith in every generation. They show how the actions of God have been effective in the lives of people at every turning point in the story. Such repetition maintains the corporate memory and enables it to be applied to the context in each 'new' year. The story is reinforced by rituals and by the songs that are 'special' to that season. Each member of the Church is therefore helped to feel that they belong, that they know the story, and how to sing the songs. The aim of the liturgy is to underline that the story is 'old' ('Tell me the old, old, story'), but it is also

---

7 See Bal, Micke (1999), 'Introduction', in Bal, Crewe, and Spitzer (eds), *Acts of Memory: Cultural Recall in the Present*, p. x: 'Ordinary narrative memory fundamentally serves a social function: it comes about in a cultural context whose frame evokes and enables memory. It is a context in which, precisely, the past makes sense in the present . . .'

continually 'new' ('New every morning is the love').[8] Pfatteicher, declares: 'Symbol, myth, ritual, liturgy encourage and enable us to find suggestive patterns in the world in which and by which we live and also see through the cracks of the visible universe to find deeper harmony.'[9]

Memory and Nostalgia

If the corporate memory is not constantly applied and adapted to the new context, the society can be frozen in the past and become unable to attract new members. Nostalgia is a pining for the past in such a way that it shapes the memory by detaching it from the context and by giving it a form which has more emotional investment than reality. Christopher Lasch goes so far as to declare that nostalgia cannot be said to be memory as such:

> Strictly speaking, nostalgia does not entail the exercise of memory at all, since the past it idealizes stands outside time, frozen in unchanging perfection. Memory too may idealize the past, but not in order to condemn the present. It draws hope and comfort from the past in order to enrich the present and to face what comes with good cheer. It sees past, present, and future as continuous.[10]

Nostalgia disregards the context of the memory and therefore could be said to be a projection of memory rather than memory itself. Nostalgia selects the parts of the memory that suit the emotional needs of people and projects that selection into the present as if the ideal perfect context could be established. Corporate memory on the other hand remembers the context of the remembered event and is realistic about the present context. The fault with nostalgia lies not so much with the distortion of past memories as the failure to recognize the reality of the current situation.

So in liturgy the remembrance of the resurrection of Christ is always set in the remembered context of his death, and of the difficulty of the first disciples to relate the resurrection to the facts of earthly life. In liturgy the victory of Christ over sin is always remembered within the context of the sinfulness of humanity, and its need for repentance and the power of the Spirit to live in obedience to God.

Christian communities that live by nostalgia cut off the present from the past in a way that a fully operating brain only does at its peril. As we have seen, the corporate memory only stays alive when it is in touch with the past in such a way that it empowers the present and guides the future.

---

[8] Two hymns from different traditions, the first from Sankey and Moody and the second from J. Keble.

[9] Pfatteicher (1995), p. 79.

[10] Lasch, Christopher (1991), *The True and Only Heaven – Progress and its critics.*

Memory and Hope

In *The True and Only Heaven*, Lasch indicates that one of the functions of corporate memory is to provide hope and comfort for the present and future situations. The story which sustains corporate memory contains examples of how previous generations have faced a crisis, found strength and guidance to overcome it, and then succeeded to continue their journey. The story of the past is able to illustrate how the community was able to regather its resources and move forward.

In the Christian community one of the functions of worship is to retell the story of God's grace in such a way that the Church is able to face the crisis of sin and fear of 'death', and, relying on God, move on to a new future. Saint Paul writing to the Church in Corinth declares that our relationships with God in Christ gives us three key qualities: faith, hope and love.[11] Through our faith and trust in God's grace we hear of God's action of salvation and empowerment. This gives us hope that we and those around us can be renewed through forgiveness and strength. This in turn allows us to exercise God's grace by putting love into action in our relationships with other people, particularly those who share our commitment to Christ in the Church. The corporate memory of God's actions in Christ reaffirms our faith so that we can hear the message of hope, and enact that message in the present context by loving our neighbours as Christ loves us.

Memory and Hurt

Part of all corporate memory is the memory of hurts received or inflicted, and the pain that this caused. A corporate memory that forgets such pain is in danger of nostalgia or of not knowing how to deal with pain. If the pain is buried and not acknowledged then it usually causes continuing anger and resentment within the community. In time this will result in the breakdown of the community and the loss of corporate memory. Charles Elliott has written:

> Some wise counsellors and spiritual guides talk about 'the healing of memory' as applicable both to individuals and to communities. The healing can take the form of reliving the hurt or trauma, with everyone contributing their perspective to build up as complete a picture as possible, with the emphasis less on the factual consistency of the memories (it is rare and often suspicious if memories dovetail perfectly) than on the emotional comprehensiveness of the memories.[12]

The story of forgiveness and hope is the essential backdrop for the story of pain, so that the end result is respect and reconciliation. The corporate memory of hurt is retold in the light of reconciliation (attempted or achieved) and this gives hope

---

[11] 1 Cor. 13:13.
[12] Elliott, Charles (1988), *Signs of Our Times – Prayer and Action to Change the World*, pp. 114–15.

to the community that present and future hurts can be healed. Chapter 7 looks in detail at how the memory can achieve such healing in a realistic way. Here it is sufficient to note that the story of hurt is part of the full story to be constantly retold to maintain the corporate memory.

In liturgical terms this is one reason why the story of the sins of the disciples and the early Church are laid bare as the New Testament is read during worship. The passion of Christ forms a key part of the corporate memory, not only because it brings hope but also because it shows realistically the hurts that human beings inflict on one another, and how these hurts can be overcome. The story, songs and rituals of Holy Week must be continually refreshed in the memory of the Church if the corporate memory is going to enrich the life of all communities.

Loss of Memory

My main concern at this present time is that, with the focus on the individual, the corporate memory will be lost, and its importance in society ignored. At a community level, migration has disrupted the corporate memory of many societies. Much migration is temporary rather than permanent as economic pressures make people move to the market. This leaves them with little sense of connectedness to place or to community. We may have a passport (or a number of passports) but no roots in a land to call our own. Because we are temporary we may not consider the story of the place where we reside 'our story'. Its community may be so diverse by race, culture and religion that there are few common stories to which we can relate. We may respect (or resent) our neighbour's difference, but there is no common sense of identity or belonging. Our memories are not their memories, so we have little to share in common. Often the memories of the individual are kept in a box of personal belongings and do not contribute to those of the community.

Corporate memories are strongest when the numbers in the group are in their hundreds rather than thousands. Once the community is too large, the sense of participation is diminished. It is easier to retain a corporate memory in a village than in a city, in a church of two hundred than a church of two thousand members, in a county than in a country, even in a nation than in a union of nations. There seems to be a stronger sense of corporate identity among a group of people with a common culture and a common faith. My own Irish heritage ties me still to a land, a people and a language expressed in story, dance, music and song, even though I live in New Zealand and only visit Ireland occasionally.

The threat of individualization is so strong that special measures need to be taken to create and/or sustain corporate memory. Festivals and celebrations need to mark the stories of the group or the nation. The turn of the millennium was an ideal moment to create memorable occasions when the community at its various levels could gather. Communities often write a new chapter of their story in response to tragedy or crisis. Some communities have relearnt the importance of ritual, maybe inspired by the rituals at great sporting events such as the Olympic Games. Pfatteicher comments on community ritual: 'This is a description of what happens in ritual. The individual enters into a common pattern of thought, attitude, emotion, and achieves it by concert with society.'[13]

Christian communities also need to safeguard the continuance of corporate memory. The retelling of the story of each church building and its community at regular intervals is vital for the health of the present congregation in that place. Such retelling will occur on significant anniversaries, but it should also be recited at the beginning of each new period of leadership. Every generation of young people have a right and a need to hear the story as their story, and to make connections with the leading figures in the story. The story should contain the remembrance of the times of hurt and exile as well as the times of joyful unity and success. In the telling of this story the aged will be valued for their ability to relate the story of their times. The span of their life puts us in touch with the span of the history of God's continuing love and guidance in each generation. In a mobile society every attempt should be made to gather every member of the congregation to hear the story to make their corporate memory and identity as strong as that of individuals.

As we reflect on this need it may be possible to see why the Church of England for many years made an attempt to gather *all* the members of its various congregations together on three occasions during the year. It stipulated that Easter should be one of these occasions, and custom made Christmas and Whitsunday the others.[14] This minimum corporate attendance was required to keep the corporate memory alive. In most secular societies greater participation is expected. This is in line with the observations I made in Chapter 2 on how the memory function needs regular repetition to retain effective memory.

Memory and Community Liturgy

Communities have gathered their wisdom about the way to act in relation to the basic events of life into the form of rituals. These contain story, teaching, emotional responses, and song. Such rituals allow the community to pass on ways of coping well in these situations: 'In life and in death, in times of joy and in times of sorrow, we are creatures of ritual who long for ways to mark the significance of life events and experiences that shape who we are and who we will yet become.'[15] The three main rituals are associated with birth, marriage, and death.

The birth of a new child is a celebration not only for the parent(s) but also for the wider family and for society. In a Christian society the birth was celebrated through the dedication or baptism of the child into the membership of Christ and his Church. This ritual and sacrament allowed for the child to be acknowledged

---

[13] Pfatteicher (1995), p. 70.

[14] See in the Book of Common Prayer, 1662, in the 8th Rubric at the conclusion of the Order for the Administration of the Lord's Supper or Holy Communion: 'And note, that every Parishioner shall communicate at the least three times a year, of which Easter to be one.'

[15] Henke, Linda Witte (2001), *Marking Time – Christian Rituals for All Our Days*, p. xi.

both by the family and by the Church (also representing the community). The Church made sure that the child was supported by a wider group than just the family, and so was able to ensure that the child was never 'lost'. The Church's concept of family was such that it laid an obligation on its corporate members to care for its children even when natural parents died or abandoned their child. The rituals reminded the congregation of its duties and the child of its privileges.

With the rise of individualism the natural family became the stronger focus and the dedication or baptism became part of the *family ritual* of celebrating a new member. The Church's sacrament was followed by a family party to 'wet the baby's head'. As participation in the Church has ceased for some, families have developed a 'party' ritual in which the key elements are a speech of welcome to the child and a toast to its welfare. The corporate memory of the birth of this child is not established at this point, and the child has little feeling of belonging until it enters the education system. Therefore for many children the ritual of 'going to school' is the first mark of entry into society.

The Christian Church in former years took good care to underline the need for the child to be brought into their corporate memory through baptism (or in some traditions through 'dedication'). Recent theological statements have left ambivalent the 'need' for baptism and some traditions have stressed the right of choice for the child. The stress has been on believer's baptism and many children have been omitted from the Church community and therefore from its corporate memory. I see a need for each Church community to reconsider this issue. Whatever the outcome in relation to baptism, it is important that a ritual to celebrate the birth and the incorporation of a child into the Church be re-established, and thus form a clear part of the corporate memory.

At the occasion of a marriage *the wedding ritual* establishes certain norms for relationships within the community. Society is still clear that marriage is not a private matter because it knows that each marriage affects the wider community. The committed relationship between a man and a woman sets the guideline of stability between people within the community. Instability in these relationships causes instability in society in general, which affects all its members. This is especially true in the corporate responsibility of caring for the children of any marriage. There is no doubt that the cost of any breakdown in the parent's relationship has to be born by the wider community, both in financial and emotional terms. The cost is also evident in the lives of many children. Society therefore still expects stability from those who marry. In the ritual it appoints a representative to preside and this publicly reminds all of the involvement of society.

Within the Church the marriage ritual is a time when members have full rights to join the family and friends in witnessing and supporting a marriage. The Church appoints an ordained minister to represent God and the Christian community, both in demanding seriousness and attention to the principles of Christian marriage, and in conveying the blessing of God on the couple. The marriage service is an opportunity for the Church to restate its corporate wisdom about marriage and to insist on the principles that are set out through the ritual. These include the right and responsibility of each party to commit themselves fully to this marriage to the exclusion of all other relationships which would damage the marriage, the care of any children born from the marriage, and the maintenance of the relationship even when circumstances change for the better or the worse. Those who listen to this corporate memory are to apply it again to this marriage and to the state of marriage in general. Those thinking about marrying in a Christian context are able to see what is required of them, and those who are married are reminded again of what they have entered:

> Life cycle stages ... reflect society's and church's expectations for these particular individuals; these institutions have an interest in defining the meaning of these stages in lives of individuals, and in urging individuals to conform to expectations.[16]

The occasion of death is still seen as worthy of note in most societies. In western culture, newspaper 'Notices' inform society in general of the death of an individual and often state a place and time when people are invited to join the family in the funeral ritual. Such a ritual allows for expression of corporate grief so that it may be shared and absorbed, and for words of faith, love and hope to be stated. In some communities the ritual is firmly laid down as death is seen as breaking the routine of life, and the shape of this ritual is required to maintain order and restore hope for the community. Such rituals allow all aspects of death to be faced, and the emphasis is focused on how to cope with death and grief as an experience in the totality of life. The corporate memory knows that each new death draws to the surface grief and fear in general. The ritual allows us to rehearse our response to our own death and the death of those near and dear to us.

Again individualization in some societies has moved us away from a corporately appropriate ritual to one applicable merely to this situation of death. Flexibility in some instances has become license to include many interpretations of death. In some rituals the opportunity is taken for endless tributes to the dead by their family and friends. The ritual often obscures the reality of death, and the laughter of the celebration of life does not permit the emotions of grief to be expressed and shared.

Some funeral rituals for a Christian have been influenced by society's new norms. The issue of what happens to a person at death is left unanswered and the story of resurrection is squeezed out by the remembrances of life. As each Christian funeral contributes to the corporate memory about life and death it is important that the Christian community sets down the contents of the ritual in such a way that it incorporates the story of the death and resurrection of Christ; the continuation of the love of God in life and in death; the hope of the gift of eternal life; and the comfort Christ offers to those who rightly mourn at the death of one of the Church's members. Unless such teaching is rehearsed at each funeral, the corporate memory will fade and its strength and comfort dissipate.

The community and the Church has also devised rituals for *other rites of passage*. These are key times for adding to the corporate memory and for society to teach and feel what are appropriate responses to the stages of life. Anita Stauffer comments:

---

[16] Procter-Smith, Marjorie (1996), 'Contemporary Challenges to Christian Life-Cycle Ritual', in Bradshaw, Paul and Hoffman, Lawrence (eds), *Life Cycles in Jewish and Christian Worship*, p. 257.

Rites of passage are those communal symbolic processes and acts connected with important or critical transitions in the lives of individuals and communities. In almost all cultures, giving birth, coming to adulthood, marrying, reconciling, leave-taking, passage into and sometimes through sickness, and dying, and grieving, among several other transitions, are marked by diverse communal rites that express the process of separation, liminality (the transitional or 'in between' stage), and incorporation.[17]

Corporate memory, as enshrined in rituals, gives us the opportunity to respond as a group and as individuals to all these situations in such a way that our feelings are given full expression and our minds are informed of our responsibilities and privileges. Without such rituals the turning points of life go unnoticed and we are left confused about who we are and what can be expected of us and for us in the future.

Summary

Corporate memory is essential for the development of individual memory. Without the wisdom of the group we are unable to learn to respond to life situations. Confusion arises for the individual and the group when corporate memory is fragmented or lost. Corporate memory is retained through repetition and continual application to the evolving context. If resilient it will cope with change due to crisis. If it fails to take note of the context memory may be replaced with nostalgia, which denies realism and attempts to create perfection. Corporate memory enriches the community with hope and with guidelines for rituals to deal with relationships.

The use of liturgy is a major means by which the corporate memory of the Church is maintained and applied to new contexts. Its story, songs, teaching and ritual pick up the memory of God's people in the past and allow it to empower and inform them for the present and the future. A liturgy to achieve this purpose needs to give worshippers a strong sense of participation and significance. The responsibility for maintaining this corporate memory lies with all members supported by the leadership of the Church.

---

[17] Stauffer, S. Anita (1999), *Baptism, Rites of Passages and Culture*, p. 14.

Chapter 7

Memories of Sin and Pain

Mending Memories

Some memories are painful and fill us with fear every time the memory comes flooding back. Some people who have been in a car crash remember, both awake and asleep, the scenes attached to it. They find these literally dreadful, the cause of dread and endless fear. They relive the incident and find it hard to overcome feelings of anger, bitterness and apportionment of blame, either to themselves or to others. In such circumstances for the Church to speak of the forgiveness of those responsible is correct but very difficult. Such a memory cannot be easily erased from the mind. To the memory is attached a whole range of emotions. There is indeed need for forgiveness so that blame and bitterness do not poison the future, but the process of forgiveness is like any other form of healing. It will take time, new insights, and much support, for the recovery to occur.

Examining the processes of the brain may provide clues as to the most effective means of achieving the goal of mending a memory. One avenue to pursue is to find out how the mind selects material for retention or deletion in the memory. For retention to occur effectively the mind needs to repeat the material at regular intervals. If the material is meaningful, the more frequent the repetition, the greater the retention. The mind also works on a 'weighting' system. What is considered of major significance is given higher priority for retention than the routine or the trivial. In the act of forgiveness it may be possible to re-weight the feelings attached to the memory of a particular action. The act of forgiveness may release the mind from the desire to recall this incident frequently because it is no longer seen as relevant to the relationship between God and the forgiven, or to the relationship between the forgiven and another person whom they have hurt. This is because the act of forgiveness has changed the weighting of the incident. It is no longer as important because a more significant incident has occurred, that is, the love and generosity which through forgiveness overcame the hurt. What is now remembered is the joy of forgiveness and the wonder of the generosity shown in the act of forgiveness. The priority memory becomes the hug and kiss of reconciliation and the renewal of the relationship, rather than the previous damage.

On the other hand the act of confession and forgiveness, if wrongly approached, can in itself reinforce the memory of sin and the attached guilt. When each call to confession only results in the repetition of a list of previous sins, it fails in its purpose of releasing guilt and renewing the relationship. The purpose of confession is to free the sinner for future good, not to freeze the sinner in past guilt. Forgiveness needs to be seen as the catalyst of change.

Theories of Knowledge Change

We can gain insights into the process of change by examining some current
theories of change in scientific knowledge. In using this research in the field of
education[1] I will attempt to find parallels to the change from knowing that I am a
sinner and therefore feeling 'unloved', to the knowledge that I am forgiven and
therefore able to enter or re-enter a loving relationship with the Other. Chinn and
Brewer summarize current educational research into knowledge change in an article
entitled 'Theories of Knowledge Acquisition'. They record that 'Researchers infer
that knowledge change is triggered by events involving new data; new conceptions;
reflection; and social pressures.'[2] I want to see how these four events can be
applied to the mending of memories.

New Data

Data is a broadly used term which includes observations of the world and instances
or examples of what happens in certain circumstances.[3] In the case of forgiveness
the existing data held in the mind is that what has been done is wrong or harmful
to the doer and those affected by what is known as sin. In the act of forgiveness
this is matched with the new data that a person can be forgiven by God, and by
those hurt by the sin, so that reconciliation is possible. Such new data about the
possibility of forgiveness is confirmed by the actual facts shown in the narrative of
Christ's passion on the cross, when this is acknowledged as an event of history.
The sequence may be like this. A person will remember the damaging incident (the
sin) and feel sorrow and guilt, possibly accompanied by anger and the attempt to
transfer the blame. To this painful memory will be added the new data of Christ's
promise of forgiveness, made factual in the Cross. For forgiveness to occur, for
there to be a change of heart and direction, such new data will need to be
introduced to the person who has sinned in such a way that it is accepted and
heard. In this way a change can take place. For this to happen the data needs to be
proclaimed through the written or spoken word. This is the proclamation of good
news, seen as new data to be put alongside the bad news which is the existing data.
In the liturgy such a proclamation is set out in the portion known as the 'Invitation
to Confession'. An example from the New Zealand Prayer Book[4] is worded: 'If we
confess our sins, God is faithful and just and will forgive our sins.' This data is
likewise confirmed in the words used at the absolution:

---

[1] I am grateful to Dr Richard Hamilton of the School of Education in the University of
     Auckland for drawing my attention to this research.
[2] Chinn, Clark A. and Brewer, William F. (1998), 'Theories of Knowledge Acquisition', in
     Fraser, B.J. and Tobin, K.G. (eds), *International Handbook of Science Education*, London:
     Kluwer Academic Publishers, pp. 97–113.
[3] 'The term "data" is used in a broad sense, which includes results of experiments,
     observations of the world and instances or examples', Chinn and Brewer (1998), p. 101.
[4] NZPB (1989), pp. 407–8.

> Through the cross of Christ, God forgives you,
> pardons you, and sets you free.

The new data can be seen as a series of 'and' statements, or a series of 'but' statements: 'You have hurt another person *and* that is harmful to you and them', or 'You have hurt another person *but* God can forgive you, and the cross of Jesus has shown that this is true.' This new data, this trigger for change, will be especially important for a person who has not heard or accepted such data on a previous occasion, so that the data is really *new*. It will need to be reinforced by some other trigger that gives assurance that the new data is *trustworthy*. This reinforcement could be established by seeing that it is working for others, or by acknowledging that the person who proclaims the data is worthy of trust, or because the new data is *consistent* with other data already known. For example, God is known as a God of love and therefore a forgiving God is consistent with that.

New Conceptions

These are defined as 'any sort of externally provided *abstract* knowledge, such as a rule or a theory, that counts as an explanation for some data'.[5] A change in conceptions therefore will occur when a new range of ideas is introduced. New conceptions in the area of forgiveness could be:

- It is possible for sinners to be forgiven.
- Reconciliation is the goal for any community.
- If you are and feel loved, you can receive forgiveness.

New data will give concrete expression to the new conception. The new data explains that this occurrence is not a one-off event, but can be generally applied and so falls into the parameter of a rule. Therefore change will occur when I accept that the conception of forgiveness is regular and is applicable to all under the appropriate conditions. This conception will find expression in such words as 'If we confess our sins, God will forgive us.' This becomes the standard rule.

Conceptions are accepted as true in either of two ways:

Either, the new conception (theory) contradicts a former theory, such as 'There is no escape from the consequences of sin. Everyone is a slave of sin.' In this case the new theory is welcomed as good news.

Or, the new conception can be consistent with other held theories, such as 'Human beings can forgive one another, so God, as their creator, is capable of granting forgiveness as well.'

Often the acceptance of new conceptions is the result of hearing stories or analogies. A story illustrates the theory and allows the mind to grasp its significance and application to a different set of circumstances. The imaginative function of the mind receives the story and applies it as appropriate. It can then be accepted as a

---

[5] Chinn and Brewer (1998), p. 103.

theory able to be grasped in one circumstance, and as a 'rule' able to be applied in other circumstances.

Reflections

The mind can exercise its thinking function and process a variety of new information. It may draw material from the long-term memory and apply it by reflection to the current situation. The process of reflection works to create a unified pattern of knowledge. We have already seen how the brain works to fit all information into a harmonious or reconciled pattern.

Many people cannot effect change in one step. New data may not be immediately accepted as true. Prior conceptions may override new conceptions. However some people on reflection may come to see that a rearrangement or replacement of data and ideas results in a change of knowledge. Once they have had time to reflect on the situation the same process can happen for those who come to accept the possibility of forgiveness. Such reflection takes into account all the factors in the situation. It is the mind's process of examining each piece of evidence to see how it fits together or should be rejected. It is the process of comparative thinking and the weighing up of all the data and theories presented to the mind. It is the process of logic, that is, the establishment of what is true and consistent for the person undertaking the reflection. Such a process entails examining each piece of the evidence and judging its veracity, and then combining or comparing separate pieces of established evidence to see how they can rationally cohere. The outcome of this reflection is the acceptance or rejection of a new position. In brain language, a new track has been laid down by which the message travels through the neurons to trigger action. Reflection may result in the rerouting or reconnecting of messages.

When we apply this to the liturgical act of forgiveness, reflection will allow the mind to establish its critical judgments about the harm contained in the incident now seen as sinful, and about the way that forgiveness can open up the possibility of the restoration of relationships. For example in the *New Zealand Prayer Book* liturgy the trigger for the act of reflection is contained in the words: 'In silence we call to mind our sins.'[6] These words follow the stated promise of God's forgiveness to those who fulfill three conditions: those who truly repent, who turn to Christ in faith, and who are themselves forgiving. The silence kept allows time for reflection on whether that statement and those conditions are accepted, and, if so, what actions should be classified as 'sins' for which we desire forgiveness. Without this time for reflection a thinking person will dismiss the notion of forgiveness as either unnecessary, or impossible, or illogical. During the time for reflection it is hoped that the thinking person will accept the reality of forgiveness and the conditions when forgiveness is both possible and appropriate.

---

6 NZPB (1989), p. 407.

Social Pressures

Research has confirmed the common observance which shows that social pressures and commonly held beliefs can 'initiate theory change in science'.[7] We observe that many people are ready to accept the commonly held wisdom on many topics without checking for themselves. Most of us do not understand the theories on how the appliances we use every day function. We accept the theories of electrical generation and computer mechanisms as true because that is the commonly held belief. We have no individual data to test these theories so we accept the popular position on them. The restricted capacity of the brain makes us realize that we would have little energy left to deal with everyday decisions if we tried to require personal verification for the most accepted facts. We usually work on social assumptions about what is true to a very great extent. We like to think of ourselves as strong individuals but in reality we act as one of the group when it comes to accepting most theories and decisions. We like to feel group support for the common standards and we fear to stand out against the crowd. This is peer pressure. Often it is considered in its negative sense – in the way it can make people behave badly. In fact most peer pressure is positive because it sustains us in a whole range of activities from obeying the road code to buying tinned articles in a shop in the firm belief, as held by the community at large, that the goods pictured on the label are actually inside the tin in good condition.

Likewise, the Church provides a community in which assumptions are held and common experience shared. By participating in a group we take on many of its beliefs and share in the knowledge gained through its experiences. This can have dangers (as we considered with negative types of peer pressure) but it has many advantages for accepting new data and theories which change our knowledge. The experiences of being part of a reconciling community in which forgiveness is shared can cause a sinner to accept the possibility of forgiveness and result in a new pattern of behaviour. Feeling forgiven by another human being in a group and working in a new relationship can be a powerful incentive both to repentance and to accepting God's forgiveness. In this process feelings are more important than rational consideration. The trigger for forgiveness is the warmth of feeling loved despite the hurtful actions of the past. Because of this the loving family is the best school for training its members in mutual forgiveness. However in a family without love there will be little experience of forgiveness and this 'social pressure' will cause many people to deny that forgiveness in wider society and from God is possible.

The knowledge of life held by a community which has proven it is trustworthy has a profound influence on the beliefs and actions of its members. The mutuality of forgiveness within the community is well expressed in these words of absolution:

> God forgives you.
> Forgive others;
> forgive yourself.[8]

---

[7] Chinn and Brewer (1998), p. 103.
[8] NZPB (1989), p. 458.

It is also confirmed in this response to the words of forgiveness:

> We shall all be one in Christ,
> one in our life together.[9]

Reactions to Change

The research into how change takes place in the field of education has some further
pointers that are useful for the examination of how change takes place during
liturgy. The research shows that there can be varied reactions by people to a change
in knowledge. Some people accept new knowledge but this does not result in a
change in the overall pattern of what they believe. The new knowledge is not
integrated into their total mental pattern. Their reactions can be defined in a number
of ways:

- *Compartmentalization* – In this condition each piece of knowledge is held
  in a different 'file' and there is no interrelationship between knowledge 'A'
  and knowledge 'B'. Even if contradictory, such pieces of accepted knowledge can sit side by side without the holder being aware or acting on the
  inconsistency. For example, the worshipper can believe that Jesus died on
  the cross for the salvation of the world but still believe that God cannot
  forgive a particular sin that has been committed.

- *Withheld belief* – In this case judgment is withheld about both the new
  knowledge (even when accepted as true) and the old knowledge. The new
  knowledge may suspend all belief in that area of knowledge. A worshipper
  can accept that God is love and therefore forgives sinners. This is *new*
  knowledge. Previously the accepted position was that God is the judge of
  all moral behaviour and when someone breaks God's law that person is
  condemned to punishment. There is therefore a clash between the two sets
  of knowledge. This may result in a worshipper withholding belief in God
  altogether. As the two statements cannot be fitted together, belief in the
  whole issue is suspended.

- *Knowledge change without a change in understanding* – In this case the
  knowledge is accepted in its own right but its significance is not grasped
  sufficiently for there to be a change in ongoing theories or beliefs held. The
  worshipper can accept that Jesus died for sinners but never accept that the
  relationship broken by sin can in this case be renewed and allowed to grow.
  The act of forgiveness is accepted but not applied in such a way that it
  changes fundamental attitudes and actions. The worshipper may continue to
  hold onto the guilt of sin because, though they believe that God can forgive
  sin, they cannot believe that they are seen by God as other than guilty of it.
  This can leave the worshipper in perpetual fear of God, stunting the

---

9   Ibid., p. 479.

possibility of a developing relationship. The knowledge that they are forgiven by God has not changed their basic understanding that they can never be worthy of a loving relationship with God. Some of this attitude can be seen in the liturgy when after the words of Absolution cries for mercy are repeated by the worshipper, such as in the Agnus Dei.[10]

Factors for Acceptance of a Change of Knowledge

Two factors may influence a change of knowledge or belief. These factors concern both the way the knowledge is shared and the person who advocates the change of knowledge.

First, if the knowledge is deemed to be 'accurate, consistent, simple, fruitful and capable of explaining a broad range of data',[11] it is the more likely to be accepted as true. Applying this to the knowledge of forgiveness, statements need to be consistent and straightforward, and give rise to perceived benefits for the hearers. For those who have already accepted a Christian position on the authority of Scripture, quotations from the Bible containing the words and actions of Jesus will be received as accurate data. The phrase 'Jesus said' will attract attention and the words spoken will be judged trustworthy. Such words will need to be consistent with other known words, and with the deeds of Jesus which show how these words were fruitful in the lives of those who received forgiveness.

Secondly, the person chosen to restate the words of Jesus has an important influence on the way the knowledge is interpreted. The person making the proclamation needs to be a person of status and recognized authority. Many churches highlight this point by reserving the statement of Absolution to those in positions of trust and leadership, such as a bishop or a priest. They act, not in their own right, but as representatives of both God and the community of believers, who are also part of the action of forgiveness. Because of their authority these ministers speak for God and address the penitent directly in the 'you' form. This does not imply that they are without sin themselves, but that it is their role to speak for God and God's community.

Belief in the Process of Forgiveness

Chinn and Brewer in the summary at the end of their article make this statement: 'Science teachers' beliefs about how knowledge is acquired can have large implications for the way in which science content is presented and how learning is organized.'[12] The same statement is equally true when applied to the Church and its liturgy. It is important that we ask ourselves how the hearers in the liturgy acquire their knowledge of forgiveness and how they can be persuaded to apply it

---

[10] Ibid., pp. 426 and 427.
[11] Chinn and Brewer (1998), p. 109.
[12] Ibid., p. 111.

to their own situation. We have seen in the previous paragraphs some key places where the liturgy must present the 'knowledge' about forgiveness and allow the worshipper to receive it and apply it.

Personality Preferences

Further light is cast on the method by which various people process knowledge from the study of personality type preferences. Professor Leslie Francis and I have applied the Myers Briggs theory to the reception of the words of the Gospel proclaimed in the lections during the liturgy. In his Introduction at the beginning of each of the books in the series Professor Francis writes:

> According to the theory, each individual needs to draw on all four functions of the two processes: sensing and intuition, thinking and feeling. But at the same time one of these four functions is preferred and becomes dominant. The four functions of sensing and intuition, thinking and feeling, when dominant, approach the world in different ways. These different approaches will be attracted by very different perspectives in preaching.[13]

It is appropriate to apply this insight not only to preaching but also to the proclamation of forgiveness. We can look at each preference in turn and see how it will respond:

- The *sensing* preference will respond to the presentation of hard data about forgiveness. It will look for historical facts and current reality. It will want to be told about Christ's words and actions to achieve forgiveness for real people. Among the data available it will be especially attentive to Christ's words of forgiveness on the cross.

- The *intuitive* preference will want to look at the big picture and see how the theory of forgiveness applies in many different situations. It will respond to stories and parables that illustrate how forgiveness works in general principle. It will seek to discover the parallels between the incidents in the time of Jesus and the current situations.

- The *thinking* preference will take time to reflect on all the issues involved with forgiveness, and apply critical thinking to each of them to see if they can be fitted together into a pattern which satisfies the mind. Those who hold this preference as dominant will see knowledge as a matter of the mind rather than the heart.

- The *feeling* preference will want to concentrate on the relationship that has been broken by sin and can be restored by forgiveness. It will look for the warmth of interaction within the community as an outward sign of forgiveness in action. It will respond to the way that forgiveness restores harmony

---

[13]	Francis, Leslie J. and Atkins, Peter (2000), *Exploring Luke's Gospel*, p. 9.

and feelings of mutual peace. With this preference knowledge will be a matter of experience rather than dogma.

As Professor Francis points out we are all capable to some extent of exercising each preference but will normally operate best in the one or the other of each pair. For this reason people will respond differently to the various ways of presenting the message of forgiveness. The writers and presenters of liturgy need to be aware that there should be adequate material and 'feeling' to which each preference can respond. This will apply both to the form and words in the rite of general confession, and in that used for a penitent and priest in the rite of Reconciliation. From what we have learnt it seems that the words of introduction to the act of confession should include:

1   A Biblical reference to God's action in Christ of which John 3:16 is an example: 'For God so loved the world that he gave his only Son, so that everyone who believes in him may not perish but may have eternal life.'
2   A rule or concept about forgiveness such as expressed in 1 John 1:9: 'If we confess our sins, [God] who is faithful and just will forgive our sins and cleanse us from all unrighteousness.'
3   A reflection opportunity (silence) following the statement of the purpose of Christ's incarnation such as set forth in 1 Timothy 1:15: 'The saying is sure and worthy of full acceptance, that Jesus Christ came into the world to save sinners.'
4   An expression of Jesus' understanding and sympathy for the burden of guilt shared by all, such as is found in the comfortable words of Matthew 11:28: 'Jesus said . . . "Come to me, all you that are weary and are carrying heavy burdens, and I will give you rest."'

The recent tendency in liturgy has been towards reduction in the number of words used, but in doing so this may favour one preference over others and one type of learning process over others. Research in related fields may help liturgists see good reason for a broader approach to the proclamation and reception of forgiveness.

Corporate Reconciliation

We have seen under the heading 'Social pressures' how research into conceptual change has noted the influence of the community on the reception of new ideas. In the examination of the role of the liturgy of forgiveness this component in change is equally vital. In their chapter 'Learning and Science – From Behaviourism Towards Social Constructivism and Beyond', Reinders Duit and David F. Treagust have traced the shift from seeing education as an individual activity to one involving a community. They note the work of Marton[14] in distinguishing

---

[14]   Marton, F. (1986), 'Phenomenography – A Research Approach to Investigate Different Understandings of Reality', *Journal of Thought*, **21** (3), 28–49.

between 'a mental model based perspective' and an 'experientially based perspective' of conceptions. The first perspective views conceptions as mental representations (i.e., as tangible constructs in the learner's head), whereas the latter perspective depicts conceptions as being characterisations of categories of descriptions reflecting person-world relationships.[15]

When applied to forgiveness it is not simply the knowledge of the offer of God's forgiveness through Christ that mends a memory. It is also the experience of the possibility of restored relationships within the community of the forgiven. The words in the Lord's Prayer become pivotal: 'Forgive us our sins as we forgive those who have sinned against us.' The memory of brokenness will be mended by the experience of wholeness in the community of the reconciled.

In her address to the tenth conference of 'Affirming Catholicism' held in Durham, England in September 2000, Monica Attias of the Community of Sant'Egidio spoke on reconciliation and the Eucharist. This is the way she describes her community:

> We are ordinary people who make up a largely lay community, who believe that it is possible, even in our contemporary world, to live the Gospel in a radical way, praying together, serving the poor together, and working for peace and reconciliation. We seek to live a brotherhood and sisterhood which is deep, anchored in the glory of worship and that discovery of our true humanity in the Incarnation of Christ which is at the heart of our eucharistic celebration.[16]

The knowledge of forgiveness is affirmed by the experience of being in such a community. Monica Attias goes on to declare: 'In the Eucharist we show forth the promise revealed in the Gospel of John that, in Christ, God is reconciling the world to himself and that we share in this work of reconciliation.'[17] Note how her words are expressed. She says 'we show forth the promise'. The statement in John's Gospel is revealed through the reconciling life of the community. Forgiveness in these circumstances is not some external action. It is an inwardly experienced reality. What Christ promises we show forth by our actions of reconciliation, with one another and with those who would otherwise be estranged from us – the poor, the warlike and the violent. This is the reality of corporate reconciliation.

Through this understanding it is possible to see the rite of confession and absolution not only as freeing us as individuals from the guilt and burden of sin, and restoring our relationship with God through the gift of forgiveness, but also as giving us the strength to live as a reconciling community. The individual emphasis is balanced by the corporate responsibility. We are freed from sin to be the servants of the estranged. Therefore to leave out the act of reconciliation in a liturgy is not only to deprive those who need to hear the Gospel of forgiveness, but also to withhold the strength we need to live a life of constant reconciliation. It is from

---

[15] Duit, Reinders and Treagust, David F. (1998), 'Learning in Science – From Behaviourism Towards Social Constructivism and Beyond' in Fraser, B.J. and Tobin, K.G. (eds) (1998), p. 17.

[16] Conway, Stephen (ed.) (2001), *Living the Eucharist*, p. 20.

[17] Ibid., p. 21.

others that we learn to give and receive forgiveness. It is within the reconciling community that we gain the trust that God's promise of forgiveness can apply to us. It is in this new culture that we can grasp the new knowledge, and change our perceptions about mercy and judgment. Within the community we learn that mercy and judgment are the two essential sides of the one coin of love. Without judgment we are condemned to a life of confusion about good and evil. Without mercy we are unable to restore the relationship which gives us the strength in turn to be loving and forgiving.

Healing a Memory

One of the crucial points of discussion relating to human ability to deal with any painful memories of past events is whether it is possible to 'forget' any memory of the incident. We have already seen that it seems possible for a person to change the weighting or significance of the incident. What becomes important for our minds is not whether the incident happened in the past, but what significance we attach to that event and how it *controls* our future. If the event and the emotions attached to it colour every decision and action, and hold us back from fruitful relationships, then it can be said that the event has taken hold of us. Consciously or unconsciously we work out the pain of the memory in our ongoing lives. The emotions of hatred, anger and self-pity dominate our day-to-day living. We are all aware of such behaviour both in ourselves when we stop to reflect, and, more easily seen, in others, especially when they inflict their inner pain on us by their outward actions. In the face of these signs a way of healing becomes vital for the future of all those involved. Yet it seems too facile to speak of simply forgiving and forgetting such a deep pain and those who caused it – be it ourselves or others. In such circumstances the ability to hear 'good news' is limited, and the call to repentance can often stir up an attempt to transfer the blame to avoid responsibility.

There are a number of possible ways of proceeding. Some people have tried diversion. The attempt is made to overlay the painful memory by creating new memories of more pleasant activities. Advice is given to take a holiday or make a change of abode. There can indeed be value in removing a person for a time or even permanently from a place which constantly causes recall of a bad incident. There is also value in suggesting a break from the pressure by taking a holiday. Yet the painful memory remains underneath until more radical attention is paid to the problem. What is required is a *process* for healing the memory. This involves three elements:

- a feeling that someone empathizes with the pain
- a transference of the pain in such a way that detaches its prior significance
- a new perspective on how life can be better for the future.

In theological terms these are the elements of salvation.

Memory and Salvation

In a book with that title Charles Elliott has written:

> If, to a very large degree, we are as we are and the world is as it is because we are acting
> out internal memories and phantasies of varying degrees of facticity, we need to be in
> touch with counter-memories that can encourage and enable us to rewrite our narratives
> ... We can allow the counter-memories to not only cut our own memories down to size
> but, more positively, to reconstitute them to form a self- or group-narrative that is freed
> of compulsive behaviour and acting out.[18]

The theory he expounds in Chapter 10 of his book is that the story of Christ's
redemptive work – both in his healing of people's diseases and disorientation, and
in his passion, death and resurrection – can be absorbed into the mind as a powerful
memory which counteracts the painful memory of our own dislocation. This gives
us a new perspective about who we are in the memory of God, and who we can be
as transformed by the power of God at work in us. One memory is laid alongside
the other and, in a process, the memory of Christ's work becomes the more
significant and powerful for us.

   The story of the work of Jesus, especially on the cross, shows how Jesus absorbs
the pain of hostility and responds in love and forgiveness. The story is so powerful
because the hearer can empathize with the pain of Christ and note how in his
ministry he identified with the pain of others – the widowed mother, the outcast
lepers, the love-starved woman who anointed him with perfume to foreshadow
burial. In the action of healing, Jesus not only renews life and hope, but stands
alongside the pain which causes dis-ease and absorbs that pain, despite the hostility
of those around him.

   Those now wounded by their memories can also be invited to allow Christ to
take away the burden of their pain by accepting that pain into himself on the cross.
Christ shows how that pain can be absorbed and not turned into hatred. This
memory can disarm the destructive power of pain passed on to others. Thus the
memory of pain is both shared and disarmed. Once the memory of the story of
Jesus is embedded in the mind the prior destructive memory is no longer in control.
This is the work of salvation:

> It is to snatch back from those memories the power of determinacy and to re-invest it
> where it belongs: in the story of Jesus ... Whether the memory concerned be of an
> emotionally starved childhood or oppressive employers; or, at group level, of wrongs
> done to my ingroup by an exploitative outgroup – such memories do not lose their
> reality, but they do lose their determinative power to rule my life.[19]

If this is so, then a vital part of the work of liturgy is to keep the memory of the
story of Jesus constantly in front of people. The story must be retold and relived.
It must be retold through the ministry of the word and of the sacrament. Both

---

[18]   Elliott, Charles (1995), *Memory and Salvation*, p. 193.
[19]   Ibid., pp. 202–3.

Baptism and the Eucharist retell the story in spoken word and acted symbol. The Passion of Christ is represented (remembered) in such a way that we can share again in Christ's death and resurrection. That is the counter-memory to our own memory of dislocation from the person we hope to be, and from the community we aim to be. Yet the liturgies of Baptism and Eucharist go further. They recreate in us the power of the Spirit to become what we long to be. The present renewal demonstrates that the memory of failure does not (rather than need not) determine our present and future life. The significant memory is of Christ's victory in us, transforming us to wholeness and health-sharing servanthood. Elliott concludes:

> As the past is reshaped the future becomes more open, for we are no longer held captive by the temptation to act out our individual and corporate memories. We are free – not with licence to do as we like, but with the memory of Jesus to show us the shape of the future.[20]

Retaining the Memories

In this theory of salvation it is possible to see value in retaining the memories – both of our pain and the pain we have caused to others, and of the story of the life, death and resurrection of Jesus Christ. In such a process there is no danger of hiding or suppressing our memory of the sinful incident. We can remember and acknowledge the sin, because at the same time we will remember our forgiveness and salvation. The retention of the memory of sin will warn us of the danger of allowing it to dominate our lives. It will often reveal to us the root cause of the incidents which were sinful. My experiences or my phantasies of being unloved will be remembered as the cause of my aggression, but I will also recall the memory of the love God has for me as shown in the words and life of Jesus. My healing will come as I give greater significance to the memory of Christ's love than to my memory of being hurt and hurting others.

In this sense it is the memory of God's love for me in Jesus Christ that enables me to recall the memory of sin. Through the security of being loved I am open to metanoia – a change of heart and a change of direction. To be forgiven I need to acknowledge my necessity for transformation. If I do not remember my sin, I can become apathetic to the danger in which I am and to which I expose others. On the other hand if I do not remember God's gift of salvation, I can become entrapped in the ongoing effects of my sin, both on myself and on others.

Some psychology has taken up the Freudian theories and considered that healing would take place if the person who caused the hurt and the one hurt recall consciously the memories that were so destructive. Once recalled such memories would be exposed, with the help of an analyst, to conscious thought and reason and to a balanced perspective of the various events in our life. The Christian would consider that such recollection is not enough to cause healing, because it does not give any fundamental assurance that love is victorious. Only the message of God's

---

[20] Ibid., p. 207.

love in Christ, even unto death and eternity, can complete the whole picture. All
need to hear Saint Paul's words of assurance:

> If God is for us, who is against us? He who did not withhold his own Son, but gave him
> up for us all, will he not with him also give us everything else? . . . In all these things
> [the pain and perils of life] we are more than conquerors [we have victory over our
> fearful memories], through him who loved us. For I am convinced that neither death, nor
> life, nor angels, nor rulers, nor things present, nor things to come, nor powers, nor height,
> nor depth, nor anything else in all creation [that is, all that can cause us feelings and
> memories of oppression] will be able to separate us from the love of God in Christ Jesus
> our Lord.[21]

Liturgy's Role in Mending Memories

Our survey of parallel research into mending and healing memory has pointed the
Church to ways in which it can be effective in such a ministry. It is the role of
liturgy to be the place of public proclamation and mutual experience of reconciliation and renewal. Liturgy is able to fulfill this role when it proclaims the message
of God's judgment on sin and mercy for the sinner. It will do this best when it
integrates proclamation and experience of what is proclaimed. The words of
confession and forgiveness will be heard well when they are clearly stated in a way
that reflects the various personality preferences of the worshippers, and when the
words are portrayed in the re-presentation of the death and resurrection of Christ in
the Eucharist, and in the interaction of the reconciling community which becomes
Christ's visible body.

The Baptismal liturgy declares and enacts the change of our status from
estranged sinful humanity to the redeemed and loved children of God, who
participate in the kingdom where God's will is fulfilled. Such a liturgy recalls
human sinfulness and God's redemption as parallel memories. The water of
Baptism is both the sign of cleansing and the sign of growth.

The Eucharistic liturgy rehearses the good news of God's continuing work of
redemption through the presentation of the passion and the declaration of Christ's
victory over every kind of death. Such a liturgy allows us to declare our need for
forgiveness and renewal, and to see that need met in the graciousness and
empowerment of God. Through God's Spirit we are able to remember what God
has achieved for us in Christ, and to make this a counter-memory to the disablement
of our memories of hurt and pain.

In the liturgy of Reconciliation we are able to be assured of the welcome God
gives to sinners who face the memory of their sin and open themselves to the
memory of God's redemption in Christ.

In the liturgy of Word and Prayer we seek to live in the community of those
who give priority and significance to the work of Christ in and for the world.
Hearing Christ's words of assurance and command the worshippers join with the
Ascended Christ to pray for the extension of God's rule throughout the world

---

[21] Rom. 8:31–32, 37–39.

through the power of the Spirit. What they pray for, so they work for. Through the message of Christ and the witness of the Church redemption results in reconciliation.

In all these ways the liturgy will work for the healing of the nations and its peoples through the memory of Christ's redemptive work. It is to this memory that the liturgy gives new significance and ongoing meaning. It is through this memory that the world finds a counter-memory to those of violence and pain to which otherwise it is enslaved. It is in this memory that the hope for the future lies.

Chapter 8

Aids to Remembering

Holy space, holy symbols and holy time are three aids to worship which assist us to recall memories of the presence of God and our relationship with God. In this chapter I will look at each in turn and consider how our minds are able to use space, symbol and set time to convey the sense of the sacred.

A Sense of the Sacred

Applying the research we discovered in the opening chapters on the brain and the memory function, we can examine how we gain a sense of the sacred. We have seen how the brain receives 'messages' from the senses and fits them into patterns which are then matched against retained data. The memory function gives recognition to those experiences which match the ones established from previous experiences. We say we 'know that' when the present and the past experiences are similar. The brain also sends us signals when the new experiences do not match, and then searches for parallel situations which make us feel more comfortable about the signs of novelty. If there are few matches then the brain becomes anxious or alarmed, sending signals that there could be danger to face. There are also times when the mind has to admit that it is mystified. This happens especially when the brain receives experiences which are verified as real but do not fit any explanation. In these instances the brain cannot find a pattern or a total picture into which the mystery fits. If this is so, the mind determines that there is an unknown factor at work, and that creates a sense of wonder and awe.

The sense of the sacred can be established as:

- A unique sense of 'beyond', a new dimension to our experiences of material things – This has been named a mystery, something that contributes to the sense of the holy.

- One of a series of linked experiences of the sacred, all of which have this special dimension of 'beyond' in them – Each of these experiences of the sacred affirms other experiences associated with the same awareness.

- A sense that is confirmed or even defined for us by other people, who hold the awareness of the sacred in the corporate memory – They pass this sense of the sacred on to us by naming the experience as holy, and by identifying that experience with certain places, symbols and times. These then become recognized in our brain as the means of 'knowing' the mystery.

Philip Sheldrake in his Hulsean Lectures 2000 points out that to experience the sacred we have to 'see' beyond what is material into the numinous: 'What is material is necessary to draw humanity upwards to the heavenly realms.'[1] Such an experience of the material takes place at a number of levels. We are now aware that the 'data' is only one dimension that the brain receives. It is able to connect such data with the 'invisible' attributes of significance. For example a flower is not merely seen, touched and smelt. It is also appreciated for its colour, beauty, texture and scent. It can be further appreciated as a sign of well-being and contentment. In association with other evidence it may be given significance as the signal, 'the first rose of the season', that heralds the sunshine and warmth of summer. Finally it may be associated in the mind with the experiences of the sacred because it is linked with memories of thanksgiving to God for the beauty of creation. Then the mind may bring to 'sight' the roses that formed a display in a sacred space such as a church chancel. If the rose happened to be red that could even form a link with the flowers at the festival of Pentecost, and the rose becomes a symbol of the Holy Spirit's fire.[2]

The mind is more satisfied when it is able to allocate a 'name' to an experience, especially when that experience involves an element of mystery within it. Once the mystery is named the mind is able to react with respect rather than with fear of the 'unknown'. The emotion of awe is still present, but that awe is not filled with fear as long as we are able to relate to the object of our respect.[3] The mind associates the feelings of holy with the mystery and with the material object to which it is attached. Such an experience of the holy is carried forward in the memory.

One of my most vivid experiences of the holy occurred on a visit to Athens for the Orthodox Easter celebrations. My wife and I sought out a local church for the Good Friday observances. We could not speak the local language and were not familiar with the Orthodox liturgies. We were used to our own symbols for this major day in the Christian calendar. Eventually we found out the time for the worship and the location of the church. Our memories of the significance for us of Good Friday, the sense of mystery about the building, the many symbols it contained, and the corporate actions of the congregation all conveyed to us the sense of the sacred. We did not understand the language but there was no doubt about the depth of worship, and it moved our spirits to share the holiness of the day of the cross and later the day of the resurrection. Evelyn Underhill records similar impressions:

---

[1] Philip Sheldrake (2001), *Spaces for the Sacred – Place, Memory and Identity*, p. 55.
[2] Compare: Evelyn Underhill (1936), *Worship*, p. 25: 'Since we can only think, will, and feel in and with a physical body, and it is always in close connection with sense impressions received through that body that our religious consciousness is stirred and sustained, it follows that we can hardly dispense with some ritual act, some sensible image, some material offering, as an element in the total act of worship, if that act of worship is to turn our humanity in its wholeness towards God.'
[3] Compare: Thomas F. Torrance (1969), *Space, Time, and Incarnation*, pp. 60–61: 'Since the whole realm of space and time is maintained by God as the object of His creatures' knowledge and power, space and time are to be conceived as a continuum of relations given in and with created existence and as bearers of its immanent order.'

The ikon gives to the pious orthodox a genuine sense of the Presence of God. He will pray before it, as if to Christ Himself; yet without any risk of idolatry, since he remains perfectly aware that the ikon itself is part of the world of things. It is an object which has been set apart by consecration to be a channel of the supernatural and a particular focus of prayer.[4]

With this outline of what sacred means for us, we can turn to three of the aids by which we recall in liturgy the experiences of the numinous: holy space, holy symbol and holy time.

Holy Space

A Place of Mystery

Our experiences of the sacred are most often centered around a place which in itself conveys the sense of 'beyond', of mystery. This can be a place of nature where the natural features stand out from the ordinary. For many cultures a mountain that has a peculiar shape or arises abruptly from the surrounding countryside impresses the mind with a sense of the holy. In Australia, Ayers Rock (Uluru) is one such example. It is held sacred by the local Anangu Aboriginal people whose corporate memory attaches much spiritual significance to the location. By its grandeur and uniqueness this rock also conveys its own sense of mystery and awe to the casual tourist who is largely unaware of the aboriginal spirituality. Mountains, waterfalls and deep gorges in other parts of the world have left similar experiences of the numinous with local people and visitors alike. Times when the moon and sun have cast their light in a particular way on such natural features have added to their mystery. For all those who view them the sense of mystery means that the mind adds significance to the data, and the memory retains the picture and the associated feelings long after the actual experience has passed.[5]

This sense of the mystery and the beauty of nature has been transferred to buildings in many 'civilized' nations. 'Civilized' may be defined as those societies that have created a pattern of communities and buildings that promote the sense of stable and organized civic life. Such buildings must have a dimension beyond the functional. Their purpose is not only to house people but to be a symbol of a higher plane. The spire of a European cathedral literally points us to heaven. Likewise inside the building the stone masons' work of fan vaulting is their representation of the light, space and brightness which are the attributes of heaven. The eye of the beholder is to be drawn upwards to see what is beyond the routine. Such a dimension of sacredness is as much felt as seen. It is experienced more than understood.

For the sense of the sacred to continue the beauty of the building must be matched by the beauty of what occurs within it. Empereur declares: 'It is the

---

[4] Underhill (1936), p. 39.
[5] Compare: Sheldrake (2001), p. 98: 'Places and landscapes of the imagination have a unique capacity to describe the deepest longings of the human spirit.'

beauty of worship which most easily assists people to enter into a transcendent experience and allows their religious experience to come to visibility in the ritual.'[6]

What 'beauty' means in this context is a key issue. One possible definition is 'a sense of harmony, wholeness, and connectedness'. In another sense the mind names beauty as the description both of completion and of holiness. Beauty is the attribute which in music brings resolution to the cadence, and forms the bridge between the perfection for which we long and the imperfection we so often experience. Both in the building and in the worship activity within it, we long to put ourselves in touch with what we have not yet been able to reach. So a holy place should not overpower the mind but should allow it to be drawn beyond where it is to where it hopes to be. Beautiful things become a symbol of life beyond all the deaths that we experience.[7]

A Place of Association

Places not only give us a sense of the sacred by their direct impression on us, but also by the way that they are associated with personal and corporate memories. The place becomes the 'locus' of our experience of the divine presence. The corporate memory helps us to 'name' the experience of mystery which we gain from the place, and allows us to know the significance of the experiences which we feel in this sacred space. Sheldrake quotes Christopher Tilley: 'Places form landscapes and landscapes can be defined as sets of relational places each embodying (literally and metaphorically) emotions, memories and associations derived from personal and interpersonal shared experience.'[8]

Our minds come to associate our significant experiences with a place in which we have gathered and recalled our relationship with the divine, and in response felt the holy relating back to us in affirmation and affection. The sacred place becomes the housing of the experience of the relationship with the holy, both for the individual and for the community. All of us come to reshape our feelings about a place as we fill it with our story and add our experiences to those which the community has shared with us. Such a place becomes the home of our God and its walls are hallowed by our prayers of response.

A Place of Anticipation

Because of our positive memories of a place we will want to return there again and again. We do this not only to remember the occasions in the past when we have experienced the divine presence, but also in anticipation of a new experience of the

---

[6] James Empereur (1987), *Worship – Exploring the Sacred*, p. 8.
[7] See Douglas Burton-Christie in a lecture 'The Quest for the Sacred Place', quoted in Sheldrake (2001), p. 16: 'Sacred places are places of memory; places into which I had poured myself and all the longings of my life and which reflected back to me the shape and texture of my life there.'
[8] Sheldrake (2001), pp. 4–5, quoting Christopher Tilley (1999), *Metaphor and Material Culture*.

mystery which we name God. Our expectation is that God will again relate to us in this holy place. Sheldrake declares: 'The hermeneutic of place progressively reveals new meanings in a kind of conversation between topography, memory and the presence of particular people at any given moment.'[9]

This quotation captures the way the mind could be described as 'having a conversation with itself' about the place and its significance, the interrelationship between memory and anticipation, and the relationship with the other people who are present or associated with this place. Even the very stones will cry out because they can speak the praises of the community and the individuals from the past, now in the present, and they will continue to do so in the future. The human mind is capable of holding all these strands together and weaving them into an ongoing relationship with the divine.

This sense of anticipation can be broken when the activity in the place no longer seems relevant to the current life lived; when the activity is not in harmony with the remembered experience; or when the place itself is altered in such a way that it has lost its harmony and the memory connection.

A Place of Divine Community

The sense of the sacred is also associated in the mind of the individual with the people who have shared the experiences of the divine in that place. In one strand of Christian tradition the people of the believing community are always more important than the place. In this tradition the relationship is to people not to place. This doctrine has been strongest when the Church has been in a missionary phase. Driven out by contrary forces or driven forth by the Gospel's imperative, the bond of relationship with Christ and therefore with Christ's community has been stronger than the bond of a ritual setting. Thus in Christian doctrine the sacraments of relationship – Baptism and Eucharist – were able to be celebrated wherever the people of Christ gathered – with or without a building.

In periods of consolidation or stability the place where the community gathered has been named 'church'. The building took the name of the community it housed. The permanency of the building allowed for the retention of the memories of the community across the generations. The presence of the graves of the dead in or around the building linked this generation of church with their predecessors. In that sacred place the living and the dead could combine to offer thanksgiving and praise to the ever living God. The divine community sanctified the place, and the place affirmed the holiness of the people.[10]

A building can only speak of the sacred when it houses living and remembered experiences of the sacred. The liturgy is the key to the relationship between the community and Christ, and, because the liturgy is continually celebrated in a building, the building 'absorbs' the experience and in turn reflects it back to the

---

[9]   Sheldrake (2001), p. 17.
[10] Compare: Sheldrake (2001), p. 59: 'The Christian theology of physical "sacred places" such as great churches or places of pilgrimage is also essentially associated with people, living and dead, as the *loci* of the sacred.'

worshipper as a continuing memory in the mind. In the act of memory the sacred is located in the direct experience of Christ in the Eucharist, and at the same time in the relationships with those who share the same table, and with the place in which similar experiences occurred. A visit to the place is enough to trigger the mind to remember the various levels of experiences there. I concur with Sheldrake's comment: 'If the place is to be sacred, places must affirm the sacredness of people, community and the human capacity for transcendence.'[11]

Holy Symbol

Definition

Our mind is able to process the sense of the sacred because it is able to connect the various levels of 'seeing'. The sight of key Christian symbols allows the eye to go beyond the visible to the invisible associations which are connected to the relationship with God. Each symbol brings to remembrance a whole range of experiences associated with a material object over a long period of time. In my research I have found two explanations of the word 'symbol', each of which captures part of the meaning it can have for a worshipper.

Empereur explains that the word symbol is derived from the Greek verb '*sumballein*' – 'to assemble, to bring together things which were originally discrete ... It is the way one (thing) really exists in another.'[12] By this explanation a symbol is an object into which is thrown a concept. The two become one in such a way that the mind cannot divorce the object from the concept. Using this explanation it is possible for Christians to say that Jesus is the symbol of God's kingdom, and that the Church is the symbol of Christ. By this the Christian goes further than declaring that the experience of the Church is a substitute for the experience of Christ. Rather the two are so embodied in the one that the experience of the Church *is* an experience of Christ's presence.

From a different angle Dillistone explains that the word symbol comes from the Greek *symbola* which are the two matching pieces of a broken shard of pottery. These represented an agreement between two persons who each retained one of the pieces, so that they could prove the reality of the agreement by calling for the matching of the two pieces at a later date. Thus the symbola became the pledged agreement itself.[13] Using this explanation we can see how for a Christian the cup of blessing in the Eucharist can be the symbol of the new covenant sealed by Christ's sacrifice on the Cross. The mind combines both parts (the object and the conception) in a single whole.

---

[11] Sheldrake (2001), p. 153.
[12] Empereur (1987), p. 34.
[13] See F.W. Dillistone (1986), *The Power of Symbols*, p. 14.

The Symbol of the Sacred

The conjunction which is inherent in the word symbol means that the mind can grasp a statement which is 'both-and' rather than 'either-or'. Much of the current way of thinking is to define something by what it is not. This is the system of differentiation. However our minds do not need to work by the system of separation. They are very capable of making multi-layered connections. The mind is always processing a number of things at one time. It can hold together past, present and future. It can use one object to trigger associated thoughts and feelings. It can accept that an object can be this and that at the same time. For example, a handshake can be a physical connection of hands, and at the same time and of equal significance a symbol of friendship, and/or reconciliation, and/or sympathy, and/or respect. The context of the physical event adds the layers of significance and meaning to the symbol. To say that a handshake is *merely* symbolic is to fail to recognize the mind's ability to engage in symbolic ritual. These comments about a handshake apply equally to the passing of the peace as a sacred symbol in the context of worship.

In Empereur's words: 'Symbols mediate transcendence as language mediates meaning.'[14] In the use of symbols there is always the element of 'more than'. This new dimension is part of the mystery that draws us beyond the first layer of the obvious to the deeper layers of the sacred. Symbols can become the language which enables us to name the mystery and the experience of its relationship. For example, as we speak of the symbol of the cross, so we refer to the actions of love, obedience, sacrifice and triumph which Jesus wrought on the cross. We also experience a relationship to Christ and the sense of forgiveness, hope, dedication, mission and identification. Symbols in this way speak for the actions and for the experiences. They hold the various 'meanings' together as bound to the physical object. Krier states: '[A] symbol essentially goes beyond its appearance to multiple levels of meaning and mystery.'[15]

Universal Symbols

Humanity has found that some physical features have the best power to be used as symbols of mystery. Such features have multi-layered meanings in their own right, and therefore are always objects that draw the mind beyond the obvious into a sense of mystery. These objects are water, fire, earth, food and light. Most religions incorporate such elements in their ritual, worship and doctrine. For example, water has the associations of giving life, causing death, cleansing dirt and permitting travel. Water therefore has the power to convey life and death as a unified statement.[16] In an examination of the text of a Christian service of Baptism many of the associations connected to water are recorded: drowning to the old life, rising

---

[14]   Empereur (1987), p. 44.
[15]   Catherine H. Krier (1988), *Symbols for all Seasons*, p. 5.
[16]   See Krier (1988), p. 5: 'The symbols that accompany the Sacraments are earthy, sensuous realities that move us beyond ourselves. For example water, the baptismal symbol, conveys life and death, power and healing.'

to a life of righteousness, cleansing from sin, anointing with the spirit as at the baptism of Jesus, the gift of light, and the new fire of the Paschal season.

Food has been associated with both the divine and the sacred community. Its life-sustaining properties form part of the mystery of being alive. Food gives life to the individual but it also brings a community to life. To eat together is a symbol of the relationship of trust and unity within a group. Sharing food cements the common bonds of fellowship with the God who provides the food and the community which shares the same table. It is for this reason that Dillistone points out that symbols 'are intimately related to social cohesion and to social transformation'.[17] Later he adds: 'Symbols and society belong to one another and each influences the other.'[18]

Individual experiences and corporate memory combine to add layers of meaning to the symbol, and each use embeds further in the consciousness the significance that the symbol carries. The particular religious interpretation given to the symbol adds to its own sense of mystery which it already carries as a universal symbol. In Christian worship the symbol of a meal using bread and wine carries the mystery of full trust in God as creator and provider, while at the same time it forms and sustains the community which shares in this meal. There is also the remembrance of Christ eating with his disciples after the Resurrection, and with his disciples at the 'Last Supper' when he foreshadowed the breaking of his body and the shedding of his blood on the cross. If you have had the experience of participating in the act of Holy Communion, as you read this your mind will add further layers of memory and associations which are special for you. For this reason Christians quickly recognize the 'more than' quality that is inherent in a symbol. Krier declares: 'the deeper, more profound, and more universal the symbol, the greater its impact'.[19]

Reference

Further understanding of the way that symbols speak is gained from Gordon Lathrop's examination of the writings of Paul Ricoeur. That author delineates three dimensions in a symbol. He writes that a symbol is:

a)   a thing in the world in which the sacred is manifested to our community;
b)   a thing which then figures in our dreams or, more generally, in our own psychic histories;
c)   a thing around which words and songs and names gather powerful meaning.

To these three dimensions Lathrop adds a fourth:

d)   a complex of meanings that may 'give rise to thought', that may feed concept and doctrine.[20]

---

[17]   Dillistone (1986), p. 15.
[18]   Ibid., p. 16.
[19]   Krier (1988), p. 11.
[20]   Gordon Lathrop (1987), *How Symbols Speak*, quoting Paul Ricoeur, *The Symbolism of Evil*, pp. 10–14.

A.N. Whitehead used the word 'reference' for the attached meanings given to a symbol.[21] So the reference to water as the symbol of baptism points to its many layers of complex meanings within the Christian community. To speak of 'reference' does not entail explanation so much as association. To try to explain a symbol is to deprive it of its power to engage with the various layers of experience and emotion as well as logic. Worship involves symbols because of their power to bridge the conscious with the unconscious, and to hold together the various complex responses of the human mind. We need to recognize the 'reference' in the symbol so that we can name the deeper associations which are attached to the physical object. The effectiveness of a symbol lies in its power to hold together in unity both the material object and the mystery, and then the object and its reference in the particular context in which it operates for us.

Sterile Symbols

Symbols can become sterile (lacking the ability to give life) once the corporate memory ceases to hold the reference to that symbol. So a cross will be two pieces of wood nailed together without any sense of something beyond that material object. Even an explanation of the cross will not enliven it to become a symbol. It is only when the corporate memory is able to invest the symbol with a living experience for the individual that its life-giving power will return.

Symbols are kept alive in the context of worship where they are named as the window of insight into the divine action that is their reference. A universal symbol will draw the worshipper towards the possibility of discovering the divine, but the reference is required to make the link which opens up the relationship with God.

Symbols can regain life from their association with one another and with a place of sacred experience. In turn the symbol can give life to the place because the mind is able to carry the associations of the symbols from place to place, and root them in a new location. The Bible, as a symbol of God's word to God's people, was carried by Christian travelers, and through it the relationship with God was re-rooted in a new location.

There are two movements of thought which threaten to extinguish the life from sacred symbols. The first movement is the attempt to reduce all things to their constituent elements, and to consider that by naming the elements the thing itself is contained and demystified. The human body is reduced to its cells and the reason for existence is explained by the mechanisms by which these cells operate. Water is explained as H_2O, as if this helps to define what water is. Obviously such an attitude to the physical world does not leave much room for the insights which draw us beyond the physical to the reality of the mystery. It is only then that we are stretched to discover a reference that satisfies the mind's search for wholeness. Such insights allow the holiness properties of water to emerge.

The second movement which militates against the effective use of symbols is the lapse in the corporate memory relating to the possible references to the spiritual side of any symbol. The rise of the doctrine of the individual in which, in part, the

---

[21]   A.N. Whitehead (1928), *Symbolism*, p. 9.

individual scoffs at the corporate experience, and the failure to see the importance of corporate worship for the health of the total community, has led to a position by which symbols have lost their life-giving powers. For example, the fabric of the community has become so weak in many places that reconciliation after hurt is either seen as unnecessary or impossible. The law court is meant to dispense justice for a society because individuals and communities are so out of touch that reconciliation does not happen. In such circumstances the symbol of the cross has lost its power to offer forgiveness and promote reconciliation as an imperative for the attainment of harmony. The symbol of the cross can no longer hold together the cruelty and injustice of unredeemed humanity, and the love and justice of a redeeming God. So the condition of brokenness continues and the cycle of violence widens. The symbols for such violence become the gun and the tank.

Against this background the Christian Church possesses a Gospel of symbols and their references which the rest of the community desperately needs to hear. Its corporate memory of the symbols expressed in its worship is its gift to the community for its renewal of life.

Holy Time

Organized by Time

The sacred is not only revealed by place and symbol but also by time. Time is one of the pegs by which the mind activates its memory function. We allocate a day by which to remember the day's activities. We say, 'On Friday I went shopping and bought fish for dinner.' It is by the time that we remember the activity. The remembrance of the activity also triggers associated feelings and significance. Because I had fish for dinner, my mind remembered that a fish was the symbol of Christ in the early Church. At another layer of consciousness some will associate fish on a Friday as part of the fast that draws attention to the crucifixion of Christ.

The phases of the moon were early markers of significant time. They pointed to the cycles of nature as times of agricultural activity and to the tides of the sea for fishing and travel. It was also possible to mark the hours of the day by the shadows from the sun and these were used as aids to memory to carry out certain activities and patterns of eating. Since the introduction of the mechanical calendar, the structured diary has become a feature of modern living and an aid to the memory to do the required activity.

With this emphasis on time Stookey asks: 'Is it odd, then, that Christians find spiritual time-keeping to be so crucial to their identity and action?'[22] No, is clearly the answer to that question, and the Christian calendar is a key means by which Christians experience, record and add to their sense of the sacred. The holy day and the holy season link the Christian worshipper to the actions of the creator and the actions of Jesus Christ. To quote Stookey again: 'What happens in Jesus Christ is the making evident of what God has been doing in hidden but purposeful

---

[22] Laurence H. Stookey (1996), *Calendar – Christ's Time for the Church*, p. 19.

activity. In other words time and eternity continuously intersect; that is how God designed it.'[23]

The first day of the week was a key time for Christian memory, and evoked a response of devoted worship to God. The dawning of the first day of the week was the sign of God's new activity in creation. Then the labourers would go forth to be partners in shaping creation with the Creator. The first day of the week was also the time when the new creation was revealed in the resurrection of Christ. A new type of life was activated by that event, and it was remembered by the time of the day, and the day of the week in association with the phase of the spring moon.

Stookey comments: 'The resurrection of Jesus Christ is that unique act in which the intersection of time and eternity becomes evident.'[24] In the resurrection the significance of the time allows the mind to glimpse beyond the now to the mystery of eternity. In this way there are parallels between the use of symbols and the use of time as aids to remembrance in worship. The associations with Sunday are so rich for a Christian that the layers go on being uncovered. These associations link the present with the past and anticipate the future.[25]

Christ's Time and Christ's Presence

Because of the mind's ability to hold together various periods of time, it is possible for the worshipper to look back into the Gospels' record of historical time and use it as the basis of recalling Christ's presence and power for the present. The stories of the encounter of people with the historical Jesus become an aid by which the worshipper can encounter the Lord Jesus Christ now. Christ's offer of forgiveness to historical characters is transformed by remembrance into the offer of Christ's forgiveness to us as current disciples. As Christ was revealed in the breaking of the bread to the two disciples at Emmaus, so he will be revealed to us at this present moment of time.

Our minds have a great ability to help us to make contemporary the presence of Christ. Linking the past to the present the mind is able to follow the time sequence of much of the Gospel record and make it contemporary. The Gospel writers would have been aware that we are able to enter the presence of Christ now because we recall the way Jesus was present to people in his own day. His ministry to them in their time applies equally to us in our time.

The Gospel writers are sometimes very vague about time, but other passages are very definite about the time of year, the day of the week, and the hour of the day. It would seem that when time was a cause of continuing remembrance within the early worshipping community, then that time was preserved in the Gospel record. So the days of the Passion, from Palm Sunday to the resurrection evening, were carefully noted and formed part of the remembrance in worship. The dates of the death of the saints who revealed Christ's presence in their lives were kept as annual

---

[23] Ibid., p. 23.
[24] Ibid., p. 34.
[25] Ibid., p. 29: 'The past becomes present by an active kind of remembrance.'

memorials to their witness and their encouragement to the present group of worshippers.

Ritual Time

The historical events that occurred at a particular point in time had such significance and reference that the Christian community often felt the need to expand historical time into ritual time. This gave the worshipper the opportunity to give separate attention to the various layers of association. Ritual time took each aspect of an event and allocated it a different time so that its significance could be better remembered and experienced. Empereur, speaking of Easter Time as the time of resurrection, ascension and the gift of the Spirit, comments: 'All are a unified event in Christ. But the richness of the paschal mystery demands ritual time during which the various facets of this mystery can be incorporated into Christian living.'[26]

In ritual time the revelation of Jesus as God's presence was spread over some weeks from November to January. The birth of the Saviour foreshadowed the return of Christ in glory, and the Church prepared for both in Advent. The birth of the Saviour/king as the Messiah could only be interpreted by the significance showed in the Presentation in the Temple, and at the Epiphany in the revelation to the Magi as representing the Gentile races. The reference to these events is made by the Church's interpretation of the baptism of Christ in the Jordan, and by our experience of Christ at our baptism. Clearly to hold the sequence of memory together and yet tap into its significance as shown in the doctrines, a period of ritual time was required. The same was true of the Passion–Resurrection–Ascension–Gift of the Spirit sequence.

Ritual time gave rise to an organized calendar by which the universal Church pointed the way for the local church to hold together its remembrance of the life of Christ with its remembrance of its local saints. Within this framework the spaces became 'Ordinary Time' when there was an opportunity to think about the routines of life. The emphasis then was sorting out what was of permanent value and could be taken as the ways to live in the kingdom of God, now and for eternity.

Time and Memory

It is memory that gives time its deep significance in worship. In the monastic tradition the worship of the day was divided into time spaces which gave the framework for worship and work. This gave a sense of the continuity of eternity and the harmony of the kingdom of God. Sheldrake points out that 'Monastic spirituality invites us to live *as if* the inner harmony, the interpersonal reconciliation, the social conversion of the Kingdom of God were actually the case.'[27]

Time gave a structure to the way of living in a monastery, and memory gave that time significance and reference. The structure of the year was as important as

---

[26] Empereur (1987), p. 195.
[27] Sheldrake (2001), p. 98.

the structure of the day, for both reflected the structure of the created order and therefore called to mind the Creator God.

Without memory physical time is but the passing of opportunities for rest or activities. With memory time gains the significance that God is active for us and in us. It is the Eucharist that helps us use time, place, and symbol as aids to an ever deepening experience of God. Christ is the link which holds together our experiences of the sacred. Christ holds the past, the present and the future together. Christ holds this place in touch with all those places where we have had an experience of the divine presence and power. Christ holds this symbol of Eucharist as bringing together in his body the relationship between himself and the whole community. Because of Christ the Eucharist intersects this place with heaven, this time with eternity, this bread and wine with Christ's body and blood.

The miracle is that God made us with minds that can comprehend (hold together) the material and the sacred, the here and the everywhere, the then, the now and the shall be. Memory combines all these experiences of God as a seamless robe of which, with our present limitations, we touch but the hem. The fullness of the revelation of the mystery of place, time and symbol is yet to be.

Chapter 9

Continuity and Change

Reactions to Structured Liturgy

The Church has developed structures and patterns in liturgy because this allows those who worship to make connections, through memory, with past experiences. It also facilitates greater participation because the worshipper is able to recall the structure and the fixed wording of the liturgy. When the brain works to established patterns it expends less energy in the activity, and therefore spare energy is available for the important spiritual work of communing with God.

The aim of structured liturgical worship is to allow the worshipper to enter into a communal flow of adoration and praise of God, and in turn absorb the presence of God and attend to the instructions from God as to how life should be lived. Such worship is an accumulative activity, each occasion building on the experience of the previous occasions until the worshipper is able to move smoothly in and out of such worship with renewed energy.[1]

Continuity is therefore an important aspect of liturgical worship, but, because worship is not isolated from the rest of life, change is also an essential aspect of worship. The worshipper is constantly linking the experience of God with the experiences of life.[2] Where there is congruity between the two experiences worship flows easily. Where there is a change of perception of either the nature and activity of God, or the nature and activity of daily living, then the worshipper is challenged to reconcile the previous patterns of worship with the changed perceptions.

One of the purposes of worship is to conform the will of the worshipper to the will of God. This requires the mind to carry out a continuing check on the established patterns of life and how they match with the changing circumstances, and how both conform to the revealed will of God. The mind will resolve during worship to continue or change the established pattern of living. Worship also seeks to reinforce or challenge the patterns of beliefs held by the worshipper, and to promote the required changes. When major changes in belief take place in the mind of the individual worshipper or in the perception of society as a whole, then this is likely to challenge the previously held patterns of liturgical worship.

---

[1] Compare this comment on memory by Charles Elliott (1999), *Locating the Energy for Change: An Introduction to Appreciative Inquiry*, pp. 33–4: '[Memory] is an ever-changing kaleidoscope that will form a new pattern each time it is shaken by the act of remembering ... We do not, in the main, remember facts as cold, hard nuggets of the past. Rather we tend to put interpretations on those facts. We gather them in a string of associations, often in causal chains with which we seek to explain our present reality.'

[2] Newman wrote: 'In a higher world it is otherwise; but here below to live is to change and to be perfect is to change often', quoted in Stephen Platten and George Pattison (1996), *Spirit and Tradition – An Essay on Change*, p. 12.

111

The Age Factor

The younger members of society, who do not hold long memories of the previous conditions, will be more active in seeking to amend the liturgical patterns to conform to their current convictions about God and life. The older members of society, who hold positive experiences of the previous situation and who recall God's activity in them, will see less reason for change. Their minds will hold rich memories which are attached to the words, symbols and rituals of the 'old' liturgical structure.

The factor of age, and thus length of memory and attached experience, is one out of a number of factors that give rise to the differing reactions to structured liturgical worship.

Education and Training

Another factor is the type of education and training that the individual worshippers have received. In reading the background to the struggles over liturgical changes covering many generations as outlined in *Continuity and Change in Christian Worship*,[3] it became obvious that the training received by the various groups in society has given them different approaches to life and various opportunities to develop ways of thinking and acting. One of the principle clashes in Victorian England was between the university-educated clergy and the locally trained solicitors, tradespeople and shopkeepers. This resulted in two groups with leadership potential who did not hold common memories of worship. The worship in the university, seminary and theological college chapels was very different from that found in the town and village churches. The former were places for critical judgment and experimentation; the latter were places for tradition and continuity which added to the stability of society. This observation may explain why liturgical changes were more easily introduced in urban churches which could attract from the surrounding city like-minded (that is, with the same educational training and background) laity to support the changes introduced by the progressive clergy.

Personality Preferences

Another factor that influences our reactions to a structured liturgy lies in the differences in personality preferences and traits. In recent years these have been

---

[3] Swanson, R.N. (ed.) (1999), *Continuity and Change in Christian Worship* – see for example p. 394: 'Solicitors were becoming active in the instigation of persecutions for Ritualism in general, [being] representative of the middle class lay professionals with a largely urban perspective who sought to control clerical aspirations through the mechanisms they understood best – legal processes. Many of the middle class Protestant activists were men of substances, but without the traditional culture and academic background of the clergy they opposed' (comments by R.W. Ambler in the article of ' "This Romish Business" – Ritual Innovation and Parish Life in Later Nineteenth Century Lincolnshire').

fully researched and tabulated in a number of schemes.[4] It is clear that some people have a personality which prefers structure to flexibility and who feel more comfortable with continuity rather than change. Some people have a personality which prefers to focus more on rational thinking than on relational feelings. For such people if the words of the liturgy do not fit their pattern of thought it is regarded as 'hypocritical'. Those who prefer to focus on relationships will resist any changes that threaten the united feelings previously held within the congregation. For them the warmth of feelings is more important than theological correctness.

Changes in Corporate Beliefs

A further factor which gives rise to different reactions to continuity and change in liturgy is the extent to which people are influenced by the changes in the corporate 'beliefs' held within society at large. Such beliefs are about the nature of God, and of the human condition; about the equality or otherwise of men and women; about the structure of power in society, and about the shape and purpose of science. For example, those who hold that the immanence of God is more important than God's transcendence will want to change the liturgy to reflect this understanding of God's being. Those who hold that human nature is basically good will want to remove any overemphasis on sin in the liturgy. Those who hold that women as well as men were equally made in the image of God, and can represent God to others, will want to remove any signs of male dominance in the liturgy. Those who hold that equality of responsibility and opportunity is the basis of democracy will want such a power structure reflected in the prayers in the liturgy. Those who believe that science holds the key to health and plenty will want this acknowledged in the prayers. Yet the truth is that not all of society accept such beliefs, and those who feel threatened or confused by such changes may want the liturgy to protect them from changes and to represent the 'good old days'. The old liturgy, with all its positive memories, is their haven in the storm of change with which their mind cannot cope.[5]

The Outcomes of Change

Confusion or Clarity

The first outcome of attempts to institute change is one of confusion. When the established pattern is changed the mind searches for an explanation and for possible

---

[4] For a brief description of the Myers/Briggs scheme see Leslie J. Francis and Peter Atkins (2001), *Exploring Matthew's Gospel*, p. 2ff.

[5] Platten and Pattison (1996), p. 100: 'Worship cannot be used as a means of guarding doctrine from criticism or change. Some indeed have written of the "hateful change of novelty" and used it as a reason for protecting an unchanging and unchangeable truth. Liturgy has often been the first fortress from which to conduct this battle.'

causes. There is a certain amount of excitement at the novelty but this can be replaced with anxiety if the loss of treasured memories is greater than the gain from the new experience. If the novelty can pick up associated patterns from other stored experiences then the gain is likely to be greater than the loss. In the liturgical experience if the change responds to some felt need which has not been previously met, then the worshipper will more eagerly accept and support the change. If the change does not find any connecting need, then it leaves the worshipper confused and annoyed. It would seem that those who set forth the Constitution on the Sacred Liturgy had this in mind when it declared: 'Finally, there must be no innovations unless the good of the Church genuinely and certainly requires them; and care must be taken that any new forms adopted should in some way grow organically from forms already existing.'[6]

I can illustrate this point from my own experience of introducing a new service of Baptism into the Church in New Zealand.[7] The traditional service was in language which made little sense and few connections with life for younger parents bringing their infants for baptism. Even the wording in their parts of the service was confusing if not confounding. As a priest I felt uncomfortable using that liturgy, and the body language from the parents and godparents showed they took little interest until the baby was named and they saw the sacramental actions with the water. A clear need for change was established in my mind, and in the minds of the people involved. Even in the wider congregation many did not have recent positive memories attached to the old service. So in drafting the new service I kept in mind the need to maintain the essential elements and to work to meet the needs for clarity and honesty in all the wording, both that used by the priest and the various groups of people. In terms of language the resulting service removed confusion rather than created it, and when introduced the new service held positive memories for the family and the congregation.

The negative reactions to this new service came from a different source. In accordance with the newly held theological view the service was designed to fit into a congregational service of worship following the Gospel or the New Testament lesson. This made the point that the baptism took place within the Christian community as a response to the message of the Gospel which expresses the love of God and calls for people to repent and turn to Christ. The previous custom was for the service of Baptism to be one which solely focused on the child and its family. It was therefore held at a time to suit them and not the congregation. If it was held during a congregational service the custom was for the baptism to take place at the very beginning of such worship so that the child should not be kept in suspense, and if it was a 'crying baby' it could be taken home early and leave the congregation in peace. Soon after the new service was introduced the congregation started to complain that too many baptisms disturbed their own time for worship. The families also began to complain that they wanted to invite non-church friends who felt overpowered in the presence of so many members of the

---

[6] *Constitution on the Sacred Liturgy*, para 23 quoted in Leonel Mitchell (1975), *Liturgical Change: How much do we need?*, p. 13.

[7] *NZPB* (1989), pp. 379–99.

congregation. Theological considerations held less importance for both groups than the memory of a suitable practical solution to their needs. The clash of needs continues to challenge both the families and the congregation!

Appeal to Antiquity

The second outcome of proposed changes is an appeal to antiquity. Most of those who promote change in order to meet their needs for congruity with the changes in theology and society claim that they are restoring something based on earlier practice.[8]

The Parish and People movement in Britain and the Associated Parishes Movement in the US and Canada[9] both aimed to restore the Eucharist to its primitive position as the major service for Christian people on a Sunday morning. To support their proposals they drew attention to the breaking of the bread passages in the New Testament, to the descriptions in the Canons of Hippolytus and the Apostolic Tradition,[10] and to the place of the Mass in the pre-Reformation Church.

This appeal to antiquity had strong theological and historical justification for scholars but this had to be accepted by the regular worshippers who had grown up with a service of Scripture and musical praise as the principal service held on the morning and the evening of each Sunday. Such services had strong links to other life experiences for the worshippers of the time. They mirrored the system of education which focused on listening rather than direct participation, and they were didactic rather than spiritual.

Attendance at such services could be seen to fulfill a duty to corporate society rather than to God. Worshippers at such services could listen, and internally agree or disagree with what was said without needing to demonstrate any outward response by receiving the Sacrament. Those attending could keep their distance by sitting at the back or in the gallery. Usually the singing was entertaining even for those who could not or did not wish to voice their participation. The benefit of social engagement, and the experience of meeting others in a 'good' place gave mental and emotional satisfaction in addition to, or in substitution for, any spiritual satisfaction. The independent of mind and those who were dismissive of God in a 'scientific world' might refuse to attend church regularly, but they probably came at Christmas (with fond memories of childhood?) and on family occasions.

On the other hand, attendance at the Eucharist was seen as signifying a depth of commitment and spirituality which was beyond the norm. Receiving Communion might occur once or twice a year for many and be the regular habit of the holy

---

[8] Note Edward Yarnold's comment in Swanson (1999) p. 487: 'So meticulously did the post-Vatican II liturgists accomplish their task of "restoring" former practice, that for almost every detail of the 1972 rite one can point to antecedents attested in these patristic sources.'

[9] See Michael Moriarty (1996), *The Liturgical Revolution: Prayer Book Revision and Associated Parishes: A Generation of Change in the Episcopal Church*.

[10] Chapters 4, 5 and 6 of Paul F. Bradshaw's second edition of *The Search for the Origins of Christian Worship* (2002) contain the details of this search for the roots of the Eucharistic liturgy.

few, like the clergy. To make the Eucharist the main service on a Sunday morning might be in accordance with early Church custom, but it required a major change of attitude from those used to listening rather than participating. The proposed change in liturgical pattern promoted a debate about the nature of Church in society. The Church of antiquity was a Church that stood out from society with its commitment to Christ before the State, and to the Christian community before society as a whole. Was this the position of the Church at the end of the twentieth century? The change in liturgy reflected a change in thinking about the place of the Church in society. The change in the liturgical patterns could also have hastened the changes in the thinking of society. Because of the way the human mind functions there is always an interplay between the causes and the outcomes of changes. An appeal to antiquity simply gives us a pattern by which to measure and promote, or resist, change.

A Power Struggle

The third outcome of proposed changes in liturgy is a power struggle between those eager for change and those who resist it. This power struggle is never on an individual basis. The individual usually displays their decision about change by staying or leaving the community proposing change. The individual will look for alternatives if his or her needs are not met within a certain length of time. Some Church communities tried to provide these alternatives *within* their overall structure. The old traditions were retained at some services and on some occasions and those whose memories were attached to the old ways might chose to attend at those times. Other communities felt that alternatives were available in other places and those who favoured such worship patterns could attend there.

The main struggle takes shape when individuals form groups to give mutual support and strength for the cause – either to promote or resist change. It is often hard to tell what is the personal motivation behind these positions. The changes to the liturgy may or may not be the root cause in the power struggle. The liturgical changes may simply be the catalyst for the power struggle. People with anxiety about the loss of significance for them of that particular pattern of worship may be expressing a deeper loss. Some of these losses include the devaluation of their position in the congregation or in the society, the rejection of the memorized experience of God, the failure of the established belief system about the world in general, or a personal loss of the love of those near to them by death or departure.[11] The change in the liturgy often signifies greater changes in other aspects of life.

I suspect that the drive for change in many of the younger clergy in the post-1960 period was due to a loss of faith in a God who was said to intervene for the good of society and the good of the individual. The experience of two world wars across the globe within fifty years meant that a 'miracle' God no longer fitted the accepted world view. Progress towards a 'better' society seemed to have a better chance if driven by human endeavour and the advances of science. Even the God

---

[11] Alan Aldridge (1996) comments: 'In part, the Prayer Book Society's rhetoric has been a cry of pain at the inroads of secularisation', p. 379.

of the Gaps looked less and less credible.[12] On the other hand a God 'indwelling' in human achievements, a God who suffered in and with the agonies of humanity and endured out of profound love, was more credible. The clergy feeling responsible for expounding a faith and explaining the activity of God needed a new liturgy to reflect this new belief. With no positive memories attached to the established liturgy, the younger clergy no longer felt able to defend much of the theology expressed in the traditional forms of liturgy. They therefore had to choose between making changes or resigning their office. The new climate demanded honesty and clergy had to reconcile the experiences they had gained in secular learning with their experience of the God they addressed in worship.

In contrast the older clergy were tired from the struggles of one or both world wars and were anxious about the dramatic changes of their position in society since the time of their ordination. On the whole they wished for as quiet an ending to their ministry as possible and realized, correctly, that the revision of the liturgy would cause division in the Church and among their congregations. They put their remaining energy into pastoral care and considered that a more effective mission than any revision of the liturgy.

The laity were also divided by age, but were more likely to be excited or disturbed by outward practical changes than by those driven by theological considerations. The movement of an altar, a change in the time of service, the expectation of more frequent communion all impinged on their deeply held memories or were so novel as to cause confusion. The changes proposed were of a major kind and could not be ignored or avoided. The changes proposed were not simply in the parts that the priest fulfilled, but demanded a committed and participatory congregation who accepted a new view of the nature of God, the Church and the world.

The power struggle ensued because there had been a change in the way authority was understood. The Church, in parallel with the nation, was no longer a set of leaders (bishops and clergy) supported by their followers. The Church was the responsibility of every member.[13] Even the sense of a dramatic divine command was weakened. Now it was God's spirit within that helped each to discover the truth and how to put it into practice in relation to each particular situation. Any changes would have to be by decision of the whole people of God, and such decisions would mean divisions and public voting. Clergy were increasingly told by the laity that the parishes belonged to the people in them and the clergy came and went.

The power struggles over liturgy for the Church mirrored the power struggles over authority in society. Individualism was on the rise and the Church called for individual decisions for Christ and a sense of commitment from every member. In

---

[12] This was my experience of the connection between the new forms of liturgy for the Eucharist set out by John Robinson in Clare Chapel, Cambridge and his later writings as in Robinson (1962), *Honest to God*, London: SCM.

[13] See Moriarty (1996), p. 7: 'Primary among the movement's theological insights was a rediscovery of the liturgical priesthood of the people, and a concern for their full, conscious, and active participation in the liturgy.'

the struggles 'parties' were formed and people were called upon to express their own opinions and justify them in the face of sharp questioning. Many were not this articulate about their worship, and decided on the basis of personal experience and their memories. In a more mobile society there were few places where all shared a common memory or experience.

A Quest for Knowledge

The fourth outcome of proposed changes in liturgy is a new opportunity for teaching about worship, and the theology behind the practice. As we have seen the anxiety in the mind in the face of change can be transformed into excitement if the mind grasps the need for change and is able to add to its understanding as a result.

The changes in the liturgy provoked a quest for knowledge. Study groups were formed and both clergy and laity had a chance to examine the new and make comparisons with the old. In the period since 1960 education has received a new ranking in priorities in people's lives. The call for all to take responsibility for their decisions has heightened the call for education. An 'informed Christian' became the norm. In this push for education it was not always appreciated that worship was a matter of the heart as well as the mind. Services became ever more didactic. Relevance was given higher priority than relationships. Mystery was swamped by demands for meaning. The charismatic movement has reversed this trend and probably swung the pendulum too far in the opposite direction.

The changes in the liturgy were often promoted as necessary for evangelism and mission. Those who came to church needed a type of worship in which they could join without too much trouble. If everything was in written form, including all instructions about a suitable body position for the different parts of the service, then an 'outsider' would feel more comfortable and be able to participate more freely. Outmoded words were discarded in the attempt to make sure that God was seen as our contemporary. Any words in the Lord's Prayer with confused or double meaning had to be changed. 'Trespasses' became 'sins'; 'temptation' became 'trials' or 'testing', and 'thy' became 'your'. The difficulty for many was that as the language became clearer, so the memory of the prayer as a whole ceased to recall the long experienced dialogue with God.

The learning process in society was also changing, and less emphasis was put on memory and more on interpretation. So the Church proposed greater variety in the words used in worship. As a result the text was 'read' by the congregation as well as by the priest. The greater variety of wording meant that the words registered in the mind were not embedded in the heart.[14] The service was owned more by the Church than by the individual worshipper. In society the fashion for variety and frequent change was exciting but resulted in instability in many areas of life. In the

---

[14] Some hoped that heart learning might still be possible with the new words. See Trevor Lloyd (1984), *Introducing Liturgical Change*, p. 12: 'We can encourage people to learn parts of the new liturgy by heart . . . then they will be able to use them with integrity in public worship as something which is spiritually part of them rather than words read from a new text book.'

Church the fashion for variety and intelligibility led to constant anxiety about the appropriateness of the words to interpret personal belief, which also seemed to be changing rapidly. Each person's relationship with God was under constant scrutiny and lacked the rootedness that secure memory achieves in all relationships. The responsibility for the state of the relationship seemed to rest more with the worshipper than with God. Education and study only added to the range of opinions that everyone seemed to hold.

Decisions by the Majority

The fifth outcome of proposed changes is usually a decision imposed by the majority on the minority. In most instances this is accepted, and the minority manage as best they can. Either they adapt and become familiar with the new forms, or they disengage and freeze their memories and experience of God at the point of departure. In this case the gulf between the two groups widens even further. One group moves on, attaching new experiences and memories to the new forms of worship. The other group retains their memories but these grow dimmer as the years pass. If they ever return to worship, the gap is so obvious that the mind becomes ever more anxious and there is little opportunity for the soul to relate to God.

For those that accept the changes much will depend on the new forms of worship evoking positive new memories of relationship with God. Where the changes promote beauty, harmony, a sense of purpose, a link with life's agenda, an opportunity for participation, and a strong sense of being Church, then those changes will quickly provide a new set of memories on which future worship can build.

Where changes cause uncertainty and are not integrated into a smooth pattern of worship, then many will feel that the energy required to implement them was wasted. Some changes will prove to be of permanent value. Others will be good for one or two occasions but fail to pass the test of time. The difficulty is then to make further amendments without undermining confidence in the rest of the changes.

Many of the habits and customs attached to the traditional forms of worship were built up slowly over a number of generations, and were so well practiced that they became second nature to those participating in worship. A changed liturgy often needed a new set of actions to accompany the new wording, and it takes time to practice these to perform them well. Some priests and congregations failed to give sufficient attention to practicing the new actions and that devalued the liturgy as a positive form for worship. The congregation could not remember what to do next and so lost concentration on the act of worship.

As the gap between those who accepted the changes and other members of society grew, so the division between regular members and fringe members grew wider. More families found no reason ever to attend church and when there was an occasional necessity found everything very strange. The majority of society lost the residual memory of how to worship. The positive result of this was that new disciples had no need to free themselves from attachment to old forms of service, and the Church had no need to apologize or explain the outdated theology. The negative result was that the new disciple had no foundations of worship on which to build. The very idea of worship and how to participate in it was foreign to their nature.

The positive outcome of the decision by the majority was that the result was 'owned' by the Church and the congregations.[15] In some places it was put in place by the initiative of the clergy but they were supported by the majority decision of the Church as a whole voting in their representative assemblies. Even in the case of the Roman Catholic Church the people saw the changes following Vatican II as arising from consultation and decision making in accordance with their understanding of Church.

Ecumenism and Change

The liturgical movement took place across the churches and inspired changes in liturgy which flourished in the new ecumenical climate. The Lima Liturgy and the World Council of Churches document *Baptism, Eucharist and Ministry*[16] provided a strong legitimacy to the changes that ultimately impacted at the local level. One of the advantages of this new climate was that local worshippers were able to experience a variety of customs and changes as they visited other churches. Their new experiences of God were now attached to new liturgical practice. The ecumenical movement encouraged members of churches to attend and participate in worship with another denomination. First this applied within the Reformed tradition and later became more common among all Christian churches. A much greater movement of membership occurred as a result, and people began to search for a Church of their choice.

As the Eucharist became a central Sunday service in many churches an appreciation of different liturgical practice and therefore of change grew. A particular practice was no longer seen as belonging to one particular church, but was part of a wider variety of Eucharistic practices. Changes could be introduced in a local congregation, some of whose members had already experienced them in another church. The joy in Christian unity often gave a very positive experience to a new liturgical practice.

As ecumenical interchange became established so the norm of variety in worship became an accepted principle. The idea that a 'set form' which constituted proper worship faded, and acceptance of variation allowed changes to be tried out in a local setting without such strong resistance.

---

[15] One example is in the Church of England where a 1983 survey found that 68 per cent of respondents replied that the ASB services were more meaningful than those of the Book of Common Prayer, and that 67.4 per cent agreed that the ASB 1980 reflected more accurately than does the BCP the faith of the church today. See Alan Aldridge, 'Slaves to no sect: The Anglican Clergy and Liturgical Change', in Leslie Francis and Susan Jones (eds) (1996), *Psychological Perspectives on Christian Ministry*, p. 368.

[16] For the influence of the Lima Liturgy see Max Thurian, 'The Lima Liturgy: Origin, Intention and Structure' (pp. 14–21), and Gordon Lathrop, 'The Lima Liturgy and Beyond: Moving Forward Ecumenically' (pp. 22–8), in Thomas F. Best and Dagmar Heller (1998), *Eucharistic Worship in Ecumenical Contexts – The Lima Liturgy and Beyond*.

Another impact of the ecumenical movement on liturgy was the acceptance that there might be a common shape to the liturgy with a variety of wording within the one structure. Dom Gregory Dix's book *The Shape of the Liturgy* promoted such an idea.[17] Again it claimed the support of antiquity to promote the concept that the changes restored what was handed down from the apostles and early Fathers.

This cross-fertilization between churches shows how experience can create memories which facilitate rather than resist change. The mind is able to draw on parallel illustrations in the memory to help it receive new ideas. For a visitor to come across liturgical practice which is integrated into an established pattern is a very different experience to encountering the same change in their own normal worship pattern. The visitor observes from the outside and the change does not have the same emotional impact. If the experience is negative it can be left behind in the other Church. If it is positive it can be carried forward and provide the basis for a new openness to consider the change in the home setting.

Ecumenical gatherings were often places where strong corporate worship occurred. Numbers were usually greater than those that occurred in individual congregations. There was sometimes a difficulty in transferring the experience of novel ideas for worship from such a large gathering back into the smaller individual congregations. What worked well in large spaces with larger numbers sometimes collapsed in another setting. Those returning from a gathering often had a strong memory of God's activity attached to the worship, while those in the local congregation who had not attended the gathering did not share this memory. Changes inspired by the gathering and introduced in the local setting were resisted by some local congregations to the confusion of those who thought they were ideal. For them to use the new practices would recall their positive experiences of God formed in the ecumenical setting. For others local identity was eroded. This principle also applies to members who move from one congregation to another and look to improve the host congregation with practices familiar from their previous one. This is true for many clergy and causes friction and confusion on both sides. The real struggle is over memories rather than practices.

Continuity and Change in Music

The previous paragraph could easily have been written about the difficulties in introducing new music to a congregation. I recently read this insightful comment about the place of music in our spirituality:

> Unlike viewing a landscape that enlarges a soul, music fills the inner void with words, visions, signs and symbols. When inspiring music is played, all this richness bubbles and percolates from the vast soul-spaces of the inner person and rushes into consciousness.[18]

---

[17] For recent comments on G. Dix (1945), *The Shape of the Liturgy*, London: A & C Black, see Paul F. Bradshaw (2002) pp. 122–6.

[18] Mike Bathum, 'Discovering Creative Depth Within', in Philip L. Culbertson (ed.) (2002), *The Spirituality of Men*, p. 103.

When music is added to the words of a hymn and to the words of the liturgy the impact is even more profound. The memory weaves words and music together and links them with experiences of God's comfort, strength and grace. The repetition of such hymns on a variety of occasions, linked to key life events, inserts those feelings deeper and deeper in the memory.

Some sacred music is so attached to a season that to use it at other times confuses the mind. Most people find it very difficult to use the music of a Christmas carol as the tune for a hymn with words appropriate to another season. We can appreciate this clash very readily. We therefore need to ask whether, in general, we can put new words to any established tune without confusing the memory. The same question was asked of those who in earlier generations 'borrowed' tunes from secular sources. The familiar tune may have allowed the wider community to participate in worship as they used this secular tune with the new words of the hymn, but the old associations were in danger of drowning out the new meaning. In the evangelical revivals, with the focus on singing, the intense spiritual atmosphere eventually became the dominant memory and the tune became attached to that religious experience rather than any secular one.

In many examples of liturgical worship, singing was the part that most engaged the congregation.[19] Therefore any change in singing was seen by the laity as taking away their rights. If singing accompanied the liturgical responses then changes in the words of these responses required new music and this was an additional reason for some to resist the new liturgy. Deep memories of both words and music was disturbed by the changes. It took time for the new forms to become familiar enough to evoke positive memories. Slight changes in words or music also jarred on the memory.

In attempting to change the words of hymns to take account of new theology or changes in language, speech rhythms were disturbed and therefore the old music did not fit.[20] The same situation arose when changes were proposed to avoid sexist language. Gradually the pressure built up to provide new hymns. In New Zealand we have a number of authors who have distributed their hymns widely here and overseas.[21] In turn these new hymns have required some new music, although some authors have chosen to use established tunes. This has the advantage that congregations only have to make one change – in words, and retain a familiar pattern – in music. However, this will not always be satisfactory if the tune is strongly associated in the memory with other words.

The revision of the hymns used in churches illustrates well the process of change. The argument for retention of the familiar hymns is that the words and music are the means of recalling a long line of memories of experiencing God's

---

[19] Compare David L. Wykes' comments in Swanson (1999) p. 239: '[Isaac Watt's] *Hymns and Spiritual Songs* [London 1707] were to prove so popular that they came to dominate the public worship of dissenters for more than a century ... It was the Wesleys who made the hymn the central feature of worship.'

[20] See Brian Wren (2000), *Praying Twice: The Music and Words of Congregational Song*, especially Ch. 9, 'Why do they keep changing the Good Old Hymns?'.

[21] Some examples can be found in Peter Atkins (1999), *Worship 2000*, pp. 179–201.

presence in worship. The argument for making changes is that the theology or the social context of a hymn no longer reflects the position of the Church. Some will say: 'You can't use that hymn.' Sometimes it is enough to delete a verse or two, but usually a hymn is a unified composition, and the omission of some parts cannot be made without spoiling the whole. Revision has been made even more urgent in the light of the changes in the use of language. For example 'Thee' and 'Thou' as second-person pronouns are so outdated that they imply that God only belongs to a previous generation. 'Man' in today's speech refers to adults of a male gender and not to human beings as a group. 'Lord' is only used to denote male patriarchal authority.

These three words are commonly found in the majority of hymns composed between 1700 and 1960. Many of these are still the favourite hymns of worshippers over fifty years of age.[22] If only new music is used this group of worshippers has few links to recall their earlier memories. Some attempts have been made in recent years to retain the links with the past by revising the wording of hymns so that they reflect more of the theology and language of today's Church while still retaining the traditional tune. In terms of memory and selection this has only partially been successful.

In the last two decades the Charismatic movement has had a powerful influence on the music in many churches. It reflects two influences in society's music. The first is the very personal 'me' music of relationships. Many of the words express a focus on my relationship with God in the love which the Spirit inspires. The second influence is on the 'band and soloist' type of music. The traditional form of church music with organ or piano has been deleted in favour of a form of music popular with the young. Electronics have been used to amplify the sounds and create the big effect. In this setting God is powerful and in tune with the age. This is such a dramatic change that resistance has been forthcoming. It has been countered by arguments about the nature of the power of the Spirit expressed in music, and the sincerity of the Charismatic musicians and worshippers. The liturgy has been portrayed as the place for activity, and this music displays the activity of God and the depth of our relationship with God.

Those who have experienced the Spirit at large worship gatherings have powerful memories attached to the music and want to repeat this in their local worship. By frequent repetition of the 'choruses', the spirit-filled have imprinted the words and music deep within their minds. Like the evangelical revivals of past ages the music is often the recall agent of a great experience of God. The difficulty for the local congregation is that many have not shared in the original experience so the new type of music is a 'take-over' of their own experience of God. In the smaller setting of the local church it is hard to duplicate both the musical sound and the powerful sense of the Spirit's presence. Often the words are projected on an overhead screen which dominates the familiar worship space and words are not

---

[22] Compare Mitchell (1975), p. 74: 'Some hymns and some religious art, are so associated in our minds with the church of our childhood we accept them without criticism . . . "Why don't we sing the old familiar hymns?" we ask, without asking whether the music is good or the words appropriate.'

easy for failing eyes to see. Thus many of the congregation once more become spectators in those parts of the service which previously they owned through memory.

Another difficulty in making changes in the music of liturgy is that fewer people are used to choral singing. Church choirs and music groups fluctuate in numbers but many smaller churches find it hard to recruit musicians. The range of music requested adds further strain on these lesser resources. When the musical tradition becomes too fragmented the value for memory is lessened. We have noted the significant place of music in the building up of a worship tradition and it will take some effort to make the transition to a new form of music which serves this purpose.

The Value of Tradition

The changing circumstances in the life of the individual and the life of the community make it inevitable that changes should occur in the activity of worship. The mind is equipped to integrate change into the pattern of experience. On the other hand we have noted the value in tradition as establishing a pattern into which changes can be inserted.[23]

Tradition has the value that it carries the continuity of memory, which in turn recalls experiences on which we can build for our present well-being. Tradition allows the individual to participate in the corporate memory which gives a sense of continuity. The emphasis on antiquity in much of the reform of the liturgy is an attempt to link into the corporate memory. Saint Paul reveals his own need and that of his new churches for continuity in his reference to tradition concerning the Eucharist: 'For I received from the Lord what I also handed on to you . . .'[24] He encouraged the Church in Thessalonica to 'stand firm and hold fast to the traditions that you were taught by us'.[25]

Tradition should be seen as protective rather than restrictive. Tradition protects the memory of the community which is then applied to the new situations it faces day by day. The tradition has to be reshaped in response to the new circumstances but never abandoned. Humberto Maturana said: 'History is a process of transformation through conservation.'[26] The memory will add new experiences as long as it retains its links to previous experiences. When tradition is abandoned the memory is left to fade and cannot assist in preparing the mind for the new situations its meets.

---

[23] Platten and Pattison (1996) write: 'We suggest that tradition comprises a process of active remembering, a process that sustains continuity in the midst of change even as at the same time it generates changes out of that which gives continuity . . .' p. 59.

[24] 1 Cor. 11:23–26.

[25] 2 Thess. 2:15.

[26] Quoted in Peter Senge et al. (1999), *The Dance of Change*, who add: 'In our efforts to produce change, we often forget how important it is to pay attention to what is being conserved', p. 558.

When tradition becomes restrictive it isolates the memory of the past so that it cannot serve the present. Tradition is best preserved when it is amended as it faces each new situation, and is not allowed to become fixed and fossilized. In liturgical terms this means that variation of some small degree becomes the norm, and nothing is done exactly the same way year in year out. Liturgy has always encouraged slight variation in the choice of Scripture readings and the collects to take account of the seasons of the year and the Church calendar. With the addition of hymns or other sung music, suitable variation is presented to the congregation. If these variations are kept at an appropriate level, and the reason for the variation is obvious to the congregation, that will provide a healthy attitude to the need for continuity and change.

More radical changes to the tradition will be necessary from time to time, but it is obvious that the process of change has to be handled carefully in the light of what we know about the mind and the memory function.

Chapter 10

Memory, Imagination and Hope

The Imaginative Function

Too much emphasis on memory in worship would cause our liturgy to reflect the past rather than equip us for action in the present and for the pilgrim journey into the future. Christian worship always aims to hold us in the presence of a God who enfolds past, present and future in a single piece. One of the key elements in worship is its appeal to the imaginative function of the brain.[1] This allows us to achieve more than a repetition of a known experience or action. It permits us to develop the capacity to do two things: to 'fill out' experiences, and to project experience forward.

Filling Out Experience

First, imagination enables us to 'fill out' our previous experiences, recaptured through memory, to achieve new patterns of thinking. It does this by applying to a new situation paradigms[2] acquired from other types of experiences. In this way the brain can imagine what might be an appropriate thought or action by drawing out of the memory a series of parallel situations. The fact that Jesus in his teaching made extensive use of parables and metaphors gives the Christian worshipper cause to reflect on the importance of this aspect of imagination. When speaking about the growth of faith Jesus points to the way that a small seed from the mustard plant grows into a big bush.[3] What applies in the realm of nature can be used to 'fill in the gap' in our experience about faith in the realm of the spirit. The imaginative function in the brain can apply insights from one department of learning to another.

To work out an appropriate action for a particular situation the brain uses its imaginative function to apply a paradigm from a parallel situation to that being encountered. One example of this can be seen in the way Christians have relied on the story of the Good Samaritan told by Jesus[4] to gain insight as to how to act as a

---

[1] Compare Eslinger, Richard (1995), *Narrative and Imagination*, p. 48: '[W]ith Hume and Kant, The Romantics locate this image-making function as essential to recognition, memory and recall.'

[2] Compare Mackey, James (ed.) (1986), *Religious Imagination*, Introduction p. 6; quoting from Barbour, Ian, *Myths, Models, and Paradigms*: 'Theoretical models in science . . . are used to help us understand the world . . . They originate "in a combination of analogy to the familiar and creative imagination in inventing the new".'

[3] See Mark 4:31; and its parallels in Matt. 13:31 and Luke 13:19.

[4] Luke 10:25–37.

neighbour, and to know the best way to care for those in need as it is presented to them in very different circumstances. If we did not possess the imaginative function we would be locked into a narrow range of previously experienced ways of acting for our response for any new situation. We would not be able to transfer experience from one situation to another. Part of the 'divine' nature which God has gifted to humanity is the ability to be creative, which in part means to be imaginative. We recognize this most easily in the creative talents of those endowed with artistic and inventive qualities, but it is a basic facility shared by all of humanity to some degree or another.

I am convinced that the art of worship stimulates the imaginative function in the brain and therefore enhances our creative abilities. If we honour God as the giver of this gift to humanity, then we will be blessed with the power to make full use of this part of the brain. I find a strong connection between Christian worship and the contribution of art, music, and architecture to the life and witness of the Church. For example, in the Basilica of Saint Francis in Assisi, the Giotto frescoes illustrate the proper connection between memory, imagination and creative art. The artist picks up the memory of an incident in the life of Christ but, using imagination, clothes it in the geography and culture of his own times. The imaginative function is able to apply the previously remembered situation to the present-day 'real' world of the worshipper. Through such art the mind of the worshipper is inspired to be creative so that Christ can be looked for and found in the world that they now inhabit. To move from an artistic to a practical example of the use made of a creative paradigm by the brain, we can see how the work of the Good Samaritan is currently carried out by the personnel of the Red Cross Society (or any other parallel group), tending the wounds of those in the twenty-first century.

Projecting Experience Forward

The second way that imagination works for us is to enable us to project the current experience forward to its completion. Our brains can anticipate outcomes which stay connected to both previous experience and current reality. The imaginative function of the brain runs through a wide range of possible projections very quickly, and then settles on a chosen few for further exploration. From the understanding of the operation of the brain gained from the first chapters of this book it would appear that such projections are like the continuation of a pattern or line of thought which is based on previous experience or parallel situations. If we were plotting the process on a graph we would create a dark line representing the experience to date, and then extend that line with a number of dotted lines in various directions to show the possible options that might be explored. In this diagram we can 'imagine' where the line representing thought or action might take us into the future.

Using this ability we gain an insight into the nature of the 'transcendent' – what is beyond this time and place. For the worshipper the experience of the natural created order is 'projected' into the experience of its Creator. This leap of faith fills us with a sense of wonder and awe. The experiences revealed in the story of the Saviour, Jesus Christ, are projected into the good news of God's mercy for me, a current sinner. The experience of the fellowship within the community of the followers of Jesus is projected into the peace, warmth and joy of the presence of the Holy Spirit in my inner being.

As, through worship, we learn to gain 'second sight' we are enabled to project some of the present experiences of God forward to the point when we can envisage the completion of God's work in us and in God's world. Although we have not yet reached fullness we can see the growth in our character to the point when we can imagine how it might be when we become all that God intended for us. Realism about ourselves will make it obvious that such perfection can only be gifted to us by God and can never be achieved by our own efforts. Yet memory and imagination keep us open to such a possibility – a memory of God's transforming work in us, and a memory of God's promise to us that inspires us to believe that wholeness is the goal God always has for us.

What is true for the individual must also be true for God's world. Saint Paul tells us that we have to stand on 'tip-toes'[5] to see such a future when humanity and creation will both reach their fullness through God's Spirit. The plan of God as experienced in creation is that the individual and community, humanity and the created order, are all interdependent. Imagination helps us to see that the perfecting of the one permits the perfection of the other.

Illusion and Delusion

A caveat must be recorded at this point before the skeptic equates imagination with illusion and delusion. Imagination is a function of the brain which runs side by side with its other abilities, that is, to reason, to remember, to compare, to restrain, to rule out dangerous options. The brain quickly sends out warning signals if the imaginative function produces ideas which move away from realism. The paradigm of bird flight cannot be applied to human beings so that they only have to wave their arms to be able to fly. The very idea of flight has always been matched by the brain's warning of the danger of falling. Such fear has still to be overcome by most travelers through the sharing of the common experience that planes do fly, and by personal memory of previous situations about flying that were positive. The impossible becomes possible only when the imaginative function works out, by the trials of experience, the further factors which must be taken into account in order to maintain the link between imagination and realism.

To some extent this explains why there is a proper struggle between belief and disbelief. Belief in God is in one sense 'natural' to the imaginative function, and in another sense constantly 'trialed' by the reasoning function. The interaction between the two provides a hardened faith, where faith is an assurance of trust born out of the fires of trials. We need the example of Christ's cross and the martyr's witness in death to find a faith strong enough to convince the brain that the love of God will stand up to the rigours of life.

---

[5] See Rom. 8:19.

Illusion

Illusion is a description of a state when the thoughts of the imaginative function stand unconnected to the outcomes of the memory and experience functions. An illusion occurs when we fail to test the options created by imagination against the thoughts and feelings provided by the other faculties in the brain. When an illusion takes over it means that the brain has failed to work co-operatively in an integrated way. For some reason we have allowed ourselves to be hypnotized or blind-folded so that we focus on one idea and ignore all the other signals from the brain. Sadly we know that this can occur in a crowd situation where people have 'handed over' their self-balancing restraints to a person or group who have taken control of the thinking of the crowd. In hindsight, history records that such a phenomenon occurred in some of the Nazi rallies in Germany in the 1920s, and more recently it is evidenced by crowd behaviour on some sporting occasions. The skeptics may point to some large worship gatherings and say that corporate malfunction can create illusions there also. That is a constant challenge to both leaders and worshippers, but the tradition of reason and realism is stronger than illusion in the Christian assembly. In the New Testament record the tradition of 'questioning and testing' is firmly embedded.[6] Fear of being accused of illusion should not take away the proper use of the imaginative function during worship.

Delusion

Delusion would seem to be a fit description for a situation when the brain is not capable (caused by some malfunction) of exercising its full functions of reason and restraint. The imagination then loses all touch with reality and a very dangerous situation occurs – both for the individual and for those involved with him or her. In worship delusion can be seen in individuals who claim to be God, or Jesus, or to have received strange messages from the Holy Spirit. Such delusions would be better attributed to mental illness of one kind or another, or drug induced. In such cases the Christian community has a responsibility to safeguard the congregation from any confusion that such delusions might be from God.

Faith, Theology and Imagination

Faith, Theology and Imagination is the title of a book written by Professor John McIntyre, a leading churchman and scholar of the Church of Scotland, in the 1980s. In this work, he summarizes twelve aspects of imagination.[7] This summary reflects most of the research findings that I gleaned from the other titles in the bibliography for this chapter. I have applied his summary headings to the activity of worship.

---

[6] See Peter's explanation for the work of the Spirit in Acts 2:14ff.
[7] McIntyre, John (1987), *Faith, Theology and Imagination*, pp. 159–66.

1. *Imagination is Perceptive*

It enables us to see things which we would otherwise overlook in the situation or data. Too often, without using this aspect of imagination, we miss the significance of many of the things we hear and see. Jesus encourages us to use our full faculty of imagination when he uses such phrases as, 'Consider the lilies of the field . . .'[8] and, 'But blessed are your eyes, for they see, and your ears, for they hear.'[9] One of the objectives in worship is to help us to see and hear what otherwise we would pass over or ignore. During worship we have time to reflect and to notice. In worship we have the opportunity to pay attention to those situations in our life or the lives of others which otherwise we would take for granted or suppress. Worship stimulates the imagination, making us perceptive to what should have deeper meaning for us.

2. *Imagination is Selective*

It enables us to focus on the key issues and the issues of significance for us. Not everything we hear or see is important. In modern life trivia can block out the more important messages. The information overload is such that the brain can become too tired to be selective. Worship enables the imagination to select what is of 'life-giving' concern. It allows us to use the paradigms of Christ's teaching to select what is important to God from what is occurring in the world around us. Worship helps us to see the daily agenda in the light of what is of eternal worth, and to make our selection. If we do not take the opportunities that worship offers for such selection we will be either overwhelmed by the excess of data, or distracted by the trivia.

3. *Imagination is Integrative*

It enables us to make the links between key experiences and key information. It builds up a unified pattern of occurrences which helps us to relate one thing to another. Imagination forms the bridges between disparate events so that we come to see a pattern emerging. The mind as a whole is attracted by a sense of order and unity. Imagination also helps this integrative function by selecting what fits with the chosen pattern and discarding what does not. Worship provides the opportunity on a regular basis to integrate the various aspects of our lives. Loss and death are integrated by hope into a life that also contains birth, resurrection and eternal life. Within the worshipping community the various aspects of life are experienced at different times, and so the individual worshipper, using the imaginative function, has a better opportunity to see life as a whole.

---

[8] Matt. 6:8 and Luke 12.27.
[9] Matt. 13:16.

4. *Imagination is Constructive*

It helps us to put life together in a structured form. Through imagination we can see how we can build on the past and present to create a new future. Imagination also helps us to see how each piece of experience can fit into others and construct the foundation for future response and action. Worship provides the incentive to use creative imagination in the task of building the kingdom of God, following the plans and principles that God has designed. Such construction is not only for our own good but also for the good of the community and world in which we live. Worship encourages us to use the energy of the Spirit to gain a vision of the kingdom and to gather the power to implement such a vision.

5. *Imagination is Interpretative*

It helps us to see what is the purpose behind our experiences, and how this matches other data that we receive. Non-interpreted information leaves us confused or with feelings of isolation. One of the purposes of worship is to allow the voice of God to be heard interpreting the data. Worship has always aimed to provide space for the prophet to interpret the signs of what is going on in the world. Such interpretation is both a sign of God's participation in events and of God's warning in the light of events. The words of the prophet heighten the hearers' imagination and provide leads to allow them to consider what God might want as a response to the data. The prophetic work of the Church in worship is a corporate activity to discern the mind of God and the plan of God for the community.

6. *Imagination is Cognitive*

It provides us with a real kind of knowledge. In the light of the materialistic dogmatism some thinkers have dismissed all claims that knowledge can be produced by the imaginative function. For them knowledge can only be ascertained by the sensory functions of the brain. Yet, as we have seen, knowledge is the product of the brain *as a whole*, and the imaginative function is as much a necessary contributor to knowledge as any other function in the brain. By saying that imagination is cognitive we are not claiming that on its own it can provide knowledge, but rather that it makes an equal contribution in the process as a whole. Through imagination, stimulated by worship, we gain a knowledge of God and God's creation which is just as 'real' as any other type of knowledge.[10]

---

[10] See Avis, Paul (1999), *God and the Creative Imagination*, for a full exposition of this argument, which is summarized in these two quotations: 'Science, poetry and religion are all energised by the imagination and all tell us something about reality, appropriate to their various methods' (p. 17). And, 'All these thinkers [Bacon, Descartes, Hobbes and Locke] were harbingers of the Enlightenment. They shaped the *philosophes* of the eighteenth century. Lacking an integrated psychological model in which reason and imagination could be seen as two interrelated aspects of the mind working as a whole, analytically and synthetically, the *philosophes* privileged reason at the expense of imagination. For them the notion of imaginative truth was a contradiction in terms' (p. 20).

7. *Imagination is Empathetic*

It helps us to put ourselves in the place of those in need or in joy, whose particular circumstances may be different to those that we share. Without imagination we would be 'cut off' from the lives of many in our world. In worship our imagination allows us to enter fully into intercession for others as we put ourselves in their place. This not only provides them with spiritual strength to face their situation with the enabling power of God's blessing, but also with the practical help of our response which our mind can imagine as the most suitable one to give. Without an empathetic imagination our prayers would be sterile and futile. So also in personal prayer imagination helps us to ask God to give us what is needful for our wholeness and empowerment.

8. *Imagination is Communicative*

It helps us to tell the story of our corporate and individual faith and experience through a variety of media – art, poetry, song, symbol and architecture. The work of our imagination allows us to give expression to a wide range of our experiences of God. Such expression is not limited to one mode of communication, but our imagination allows us to speak from God, to God, and of God in many ways. Worship has given Christians ample scope for such expression, and because worship is always expressed in multi-media form it is the more effective. The imagination in worship is stimulated by art and music, word and symbol, silence and sacrament. Attempts to restrict such variety, such as the Puritan destruction of art and symbol, has usually been short lived, though it does enormous damage to those trying to worship at the time. Because imagination is communicative, our faith and devotion can be expressed in every way that imagination suggests to us.

9. *Imagination is Contemporanizing*

It allows us to make the past present, and the future foreseen now. Imagination gives us the opportunity for anamnesis and eschatology. Imagination allows us to remember the earlier times and foresee the end times even though we live and act in the present. Throughout this book we have noted how the brain of the worshipper allows this unique opportunity to combine the past, the present and the future. Through worship our imagination permits these three time sequences to be held together in the eternal 'now' of God. Worship also helps us to make contemporary the lives of the saints of every generation so that in worship we can have a sense that we are present with the whole Church of God.

10. *Equally Imagination is Conspatializing*

What imagination can do with time, it can also do with space. It allows us to make the absent present, and the far away near. This gives the worshipper a new insight about the world-wide mission of the Church, and a new conception of the presence of the resurrected in a time of grief. With imagination the worshipper is enabled to envisage the actions of Jesus in one place as now possible in their space. In worship imagination allows space not to be a barrier to presence. This is important for the reading of Scripture,[11] the prayers of intercession, and the celebration of the sacraments.

11. *Imagination is Evaluative*

It helps us to put together a system of values, faith and commitment which gives significance to our lives. In worship we see ourselves as living by our values and committed to our goals. We not only gain a vision of the future, we also know how we can be involved in bringing the vision to fruition. Through worship we learn to entrust our lives into the hands of God who in turn invites us to commit ourselves to the creation of the kingdom of God. In worship we are shaped by the communal values that are shared. In worship we are intertwined in the faith which gives us a sense of purpose and assurance that our lives are valuable to God. In worship we find ourselves renewed in commitment to God's purposes for ourselves and others.

12. *Imagination is Ecumenical*

It allows us to engage in a dialogue with the world as a whole. Through imagination we can see ourselves as part of a larger enterprise which touches all Christian people, and beyond that to the final purposes of God for all people. Because of the other aspects of imagination that we have already mentioned we are enabled to commit ourselves to and communicate with a world-wide enterprise. Worship allows us to have a foretaste of how this works. The fellowship of the local congregation, the sharing of a common vision, the commitment to common goals, prepares us for the larger fellowship on a global scale. Worship always aims to enlarge our vision and our experiences. It pulls us beyond the selfish and narrow to interact with others who are our fellow pilgrims on the journey to implement Christ's rule throughout the world.

McIntyre's summary has allowed us to see clearly the connections between worship and imagination, and the interrelation between all the twelve aspects of imagination that he identifies.

Religious Imagination

Garrett Green writes of a religious imagination whose function is

> to tell us what the world is like in its broadest and deepest sense . . . [I]f imagination is the human ability to perceive and represent likeness (the paradigmatic faculty), religions employ that ability in the service of cosmic orientation, rendering the world accessible to

---

[11] See Avis (1999), p. 50: 'The language of the Bible is the language of sanctified imagination.'

the imagination of their adherents in such a way that its ultimate nature, value, and destiny are made manifest.[12]

Green affirms that religious imagination not only helps us to be in touch with the 'ultimate' and therefore transcendent aspects of life, but also with God, the ultimate transcendent Being:

> Hearing the Word of God enables us to imagine God – that is, to 'see' him without *seeing* him. The ear is the organ of faith, the eye is reserved for the Eschaton. In this life 'we walk by faith, not by sight' (2 Cor.5,7) since 'faith is the assurance of things hoped for, the conviction of things not seen' (Heb.11,1).[13]

Imagination and Prayer

In worship one of the main opportunities to use the imaginative faculty is during personal prayer. In the Christian tradition prayer has had contemplative, ascetic, creative and sacramental components. All these rely substantially on a developed imagination in the disciple who prays well.

Contemplative Prayer

The art of contemplation allows us to 'see' God and the purposes of God with insights that are greater than sensory sight. The one at prayer waits in the presence of God, and through imagination enjoys God's company and the relationship of faith, love and commitment. At the same time those who pray gain new insights into the nature of self and the world situations of which they become aware. There is a sense that the Spirit of God reaches out to the spirit of the one at prayer to permit two-way communication. This provides a totally radical view point on the world. Maria Harris describes it thus: 'Imagination characteristically looks at reality from the reversed, unnoticed side; as such, it is the mind's glory, the ample fullness of intelligence, rather than the thinness of reason alone.'[14] And, 'A religious perspective is a way to value, to approach a human activity from a particular angle of vision, where the particularity leads to certain choices.'[15]

Contemplative prayer allows us to develop such a capacity and provides the space to let the Spirit work in us to communicate with God and to listen to God.

Ascetic Prayer

The art of ascetic prayer develops in us the necessary detachment and discipline to be focused and interpretative about our Christian life. Imagination provides us with the possibilities of how to act for the future. Such prayer gives us the time to

---

[12] Green, Garrett (1989), *Imagining God*, p. 79.
[13] Ibid., p. 98.
[14] Harris, Maria (1987), *Teaching and Religious Imagination*, p. 9.
[15] Harris (1987), pp. 10–11.

discern the truth and to formulate courses of action. The detachment and discipline of this type of prayer allows our imagination to pick up the clues for right action to occur. Without such prayer we are often too engaged and on top of the issues. One of the reasons for the growing popularity of spiritual retreats is that they give us due time in a detached situation to discern the truth. In this 'discerning' we are called in prayer to exercise the imagination of the dedicated disciple. The path ahead will be a paradigm of the cross and the resurrection. Ascetic prayer by its very nature encourages us to choose the way of the cross that leads to glory, rather than the easy way that leads to shame for the Christian disciple.

Creative Prayer

The art of creative prayer develops in us an imagination which not only discerns the journey for the pilgrim but also the means of carrying out the chosen plan. Creative prayer uses the imagination to formulate the action plan to achieve the established goals. Prayer is not simply a matter of sharing plans with God, it also draws on our creative energies, gifted by God, in order to be equipped for action. The inner eye of imagination is able to envisage the particular action by which the plan is to be fulfilled. With a memory of the Spirit of God as the breath of creation in Genesis 2:7, some at prayer use the action of inhaling breath as a symbol of receiving God's empowerment for the chosen task.

Sacramental Prayer

The art of sacramental prayer enables us to link the outward form of the sacrament to the inner significance of its spiritual meaning in such a way that the holy is mediated to the one at prayer. In this way the communicative aspect of the imagination facilitates communion between the one at prayer and God. Sacramental prayer is not restricted to participation in the dominical sacraments of Baptism and Eucharist. Sacramental prayer is able to extend the use of imagination to many Christian symbols. To touch the cross, to light a candle, to kneel in adoration, to lie prone in commitment and humility, to contemplate the beauty of a flower or leaf, are all forms of sacramental praying. Religious imagination is required to let the eye pass from the material to the spiritual in such a way that the divine becomes tangible, and the relationship between the one at prayer and God is deepened.

What Avis says about liturgy in general can be said even more about imaginative personal prayer:

> The touchstone of liturgy is its imaginative adequacy. In its height and depths, its profundity and simplicity, liturgy must be commensurate with our most treasured moments of knowing that we are in touch with a reality that is unconditional, infinite and eternal – and, moreover, is the source of our deepest well-being. Human religious experience typically speaks of such moments in metaphor, symbol and myth. Liturgy needs to acknowledge this.[16]

---

[16] Avis (1999), pp. 6–7.

Imagination and the Holy Spirit

Many see a close connection between the imaginative function in the brain and the work of the Holy Spirit. The Spirit is described as the inspirer, the guide, the comforter, the sender of divine imperatives. McIntyre has declared: '[T]he Holy Spirit is God's imagination let loose and working with all the freedom of God in the world, and in the lives, the words and actions, of men and women of our times.'[17] Such a claim is supported by the famous First Testament quotation from Joel (2:28–29), which is repeated by the writer of the Book of Acts (2:17–21) in the description of events at Pentecost:

> Then afterwards I will pour out my spirit on all flesh,
> your sons and your daughters shall prophesy,
> your old men shall dream dreams,
> and your young men shall see visions.

The imaginative function of the brain is closely connected with the concept of visions and dreams. Saint Paul clarifies that the Spirit that inspires visions is connected to both wisdom and knowledge, and the ability to communicate the same:

> To one is given through the Spirit the utterance of wisdom,
> and to another the utterance of knowledge according to the same Spirit.[18]

Obviously Paul was at pains to dispel any idea that the Spirit produced illusions. Instead it bestows the gift of imagination which stays in touch with reason and produces real knowledge. McIntyre affirms that '[The Holy Spirit] imparts to us the gift of imagination which enables us to be totally open and receptive, both to what is going on around us and also to what the sequel to that present situation might be.'[19] Such a claim interprets the words of Paul to the Corinthians as he tries to indicate how we reach a new wisdom through the work of the Spirit: 'Those who are spiritual discern all things, and they are themselves subject to no one else's scrutiny. "For who has known the mind of the Lord so as to instruct him?" But we have the mind of Christ.'[20]

Paul's claim here to have the 'mind of Christ' is to be seen as based on the gift of the Spirit. It is the gift of the Spirit that enables our mind to have the insights so that we can claim to formulate the mind of Christ on a situation. God's imagination speaks to our imagination so that we can discern the plan of God for ourselves and all creation.

---

[17] McIntyre (1987), p. 64.

[18] 1 Cor. 12:8.

[19] McIntyre (1987), p. 75.

[20] 1 Cor. 2:15–16 and Young, Robert (1979), *Religious Imagination – God's Gift to Prophets and Preachers*, p. 39: 'The wind of the Spirit is the creativity that blows through our minds . . . In the Spirit according to Paul – and with a great deal of wonder – we actually have the mind of Christ.'

Imagination and Hope

Imagination creates a vision for the future which in turn sustains our hope to fulfill that vision. One of the key purposes of liturgy is to formulate a vision and to impart a sense of hope that it will be accomplished. Walter Brueggemann warned us back in 1987 that 'We are in a season when *the urge for order* seems nearly to squeeze out *the voice of hope*' (original emphasis).[21] For many people the situation is the same today, so the responsibility still rests with the Christian community to raise the voice of hope during worship.

Brueggemann outlines five elements of hope which illustrate the connection between memory, imagination, and hope:

1 Hope is based on trust in God who makes promises and keeps them. It is memory that keeps alive the record of God's promise and faithfulness in the past. In worship such a memory is reawakened by the witness of Scripture and the testimony of the faithful. The story of God's faithfulness in every generation is the good news which is at the heart of Christian worship. Brueggemann tells us that 'This is a message that transforms reality.'[22]

2 Hope is based on the prophetic vision for the future. The Spirit of God has been gifted to the Church in worship so that it has the imaginative insight to foresee what God is creating afresh in the world of tomorrow: 'The dream of God and the hope of Israel are for the establishment of a new social order which will embody peace, justice, freedom, equity, and well being.'[23] Such a vision is fleshed out in the act of worship so that the imagination of the worshipper can see the options for its implementation in part in the particular time and place known to the worshippers. The prophetic vision is formulated in the imagination along with plans for its embodiment in real situations.

3 Such a hope is not simply for the present but also for the final accomplishment of God's full purpose. As such this hope is apocalyptic hope. This kind of hope is portrayed in the language of poetry. It is the role of the imaginative function in the worshipper to interpret the poetic form and not to be confused about its meaning. Such a vision of hope cannot be expressed in another kind of language: 'The biblical way of hope is to dream large dreams about the powerful purposes of God, but they are not designs, blueprints, or programs. To make them such is to deny God's free governance for the future.'[24]

4 Hope is expressed in worship in the metaphor of the kingdom of God. The metaphor contains a paradigm of reality. It expresses in a variety of forms the way the rule of God will shake the foundations of the powerful of this world in order to bring in a new set of radical values. This appeals to the evaluative

---

[21] Brueggemann, Walter (1987), *Hope within History*, p. 73.
[22] Ibid., p. 73.
[23] Ibid., p. 75.
[24] Ibid., p. 77.

nature of imagination. Because the metaphor promises that God will govern with a new set of values, it gives hope to the powerless and those bereft of hope. The cheers that ring out in response to the metaphor in worship come from those who see their need for new life, and not from those who feel comfortable in the position they have achieved in life. The metaphor is good news for the 'poor' and disturbing news for the 'self-assured'. Jesus both proclaims the kingdom and lives the kingdom. His words and actions stir our imagination in worship as we gain reverse insights about the world and renewed incentive to act with his Spirit. The record that he implemented the kingdom in his own life and times, and then through the disciples of all ages, sustains our hope.

5   The hope that the kingdom was embodied in the Messiah, the coming one, allows the imagination to project that line of knowledge forward into the present and the future. The Messiah who came promises to come again in glory, for in the presence of God's own being the kingdom will reach its final fulfillment. For Christians the hope of this coming is sustained by the memory of the past and by the vision for the future. Such a hope is kept alive in the faith communities who 'live in the passionate and profound hope that the world will become the world God intends, the world for which we yearn'.[25] Even though this hope still lies in the future the discernment of the imagination can see how we have a foretaste of its glory within the Christian community around us. Lives are transformed, fellowship gives new expression to love, forgiveness is practiced and peace grows from reconciliation. The vision of the future is kept strong by the signs of the breaking in of the kingdom into the lives of those around us now. In worship such signs are underlined in memory, word, sacrament and action.

Imaginative Worship

Memorable and imaginative worship is the aim of all liturgy. Through its stable structures worship should be able to draw on many memories from the past, and at the same time excite the imagination to find the pathway into the future. Worship allows the creative powers of the Spirit to keep us in touch with the creative activity of God. Imagination links these two sides of worship: 'The mystery of imagination points to and reflects the mystery of God. As Coleridge (and others) suggested, human creativity is an echo, a spark, of the divine creativity that it poured out in the plenitude of creation.'[26]

So if the aim of worship is to enable us to enter and enjoy the presence of God, then worship needs to be imaginative. The human imagination can be exercised by the stimulation of word, art, music, and drama – all of which are part of a well-celebrated liturgy. The imagination is stimulated especially by the use of sacramen-

[25]   Ibid., p. 79.
[26]   Avis (1999), p. ix.

tal symbols. Symbols allow us to exercise that 'reverse-sided' insight which sees things that we otherwise would not notice and from a new perspective. Thus the bread of the Eucharistic table is perceived as the manna of God's gift from heaven to the hungry, as the broken bread of Christ's body on the cross, as the resurrection feast on the lake shore at Galilee, as the fellowship of the shared meal of this community, and as the sign of the care that must be extended to the hungry of the day who need to be fed by the Church. It is the faculty of the imagination that sees the bread in all these different ways. It is the task of liturgy to keep such a wide vision always before the worshippers.

Our emotions interact with our imagination so that feelings are added to the interpretation, the vision and the subsequent actions of love: 'Complex emotions such as praise, gratitude, sorrow, and joy become religious feelings because they are cultivated in the context of specific symbols and practices.'[27]

Thus the aim of liturgy is to catch up the worshippers' feelings, memories and imagination in such a way that they can enter into the ultimate mystery of God, and find a new type of knowledge of God. Such worship needs to be heavenly in the proper sense of that word – a worship that places us firmly within the kingdom of God. There we are sustained in our hope and empowered in our action to fulfill the purpose of being human: to offer the sacrifice of praise and service with lives committed to the fulfillment of God's mission to the world. That involves its reconciliation and harmony with all that brings wholeness and peace. Such a goal can only be stated in the poetic language of liturgy, the language of imagination:

> The language of liturgy is poetry rather than prose: it is the product of Christian imagination that has been chastened and shaped by the liturgical and doctrinal tradition. Like any artistic creation, liturgy results from the creative interaction between the imaginative vision of the artist and the disciplined energy of the tradition.[28]

Tradition retains the memory, the poetry of the imagination throws light upon words, and the hope for the future is sustained in symbol and in song as we long for the final judgment and mercy of God for ourselves and for our world.

---

[27] Cooey, Paula M. (1994), *Religious Imagination and the Body*, p. 47.
[28] Avis (1999), p. 85.

Conclusion

Practical Issues for Liturgy

In this Conclusion I record a summary of the practical issues that arise from this research into the working of the brain and the memory function. They are listed under the relevant chapter. Throughout the book I have tried to apply my findings to the practical situations that arise for those involved in the composition and practice of liturgy. In this Conclusion I have set down in a brief, structured form the major points that have arisen. I hope that the list provides a useful set of principles and objectives for those engaged in the art of worship. It is important that readers refer to the full material in the main chapters so that they can see the connection between these practical outcomes and the theory of how the brain and the memory function operate in the various aspects of liturgy covered in this book.

Chapter 1 – Using the Brain in Liturgy

- Liturgy needs to follow patterns, form linkages, and allow for the associations of ideas. Set patterns will be most useful in situations of crisis and stress, so that least energy is used in sharing in worship. On more settled occasions there is more creative energy in the brain and this permits greater creativity.
- Liturgy needs to give space for the influence of emotion and sense stimulation. This adds continuing 'colour' to the set material, and enlivens the brain's reception. The more senses involved in the act of worship, the stronger the impression on the brain. Rhythm also adds desired colour to words and aids the retention factor.
- Liturgy needs to recognize the desire for completion in the brain and its basic sense of inquiry. This will result in an ability to see the broad picture, and there will be pleasure when there is a balance between familiarity and novelty. Liturgy needs to be 'rounded off' to achieve a final cadence as with a good tune.
- Liturgy needs to recognize the brain's ability to combine time zones so that the past and the future can also be experienced as present. Liturgy is therefore able to build on past experiences and create new experiences which will sustain the worshipper for the future pilgrimage.
- Liturgy needs to note the mind's desire to link information with activity. What is said about the Being of God can be best expressed in active verbs rather than static nouns. The information heard can be expected to be processed by the brain into actions required.
- Liturgy needs to indicate the significance for the worshipper of what is said and done during worship. There should be clear messages about the value

of the information to the receiver. This will lead the worshipper to establish patterns of choice of behaviour which will guide future action.

- Liturgy needs to be composed with progressive steps that follow logical moves from one point to another, and reach satisfying conclusions and a sense of preparation for the next step.

Chapter 2 – Using the Memory in Liturgy

- Liturgy needs to note that the human mind is wired to imitate. Those conducting the liturgy must be aware that they are the 'models' for the participants. Newer members of the congregation will learn how to worship from the examples set by the more established members. Good patterns of liturgical experience need to be laid down from the start as it is more difficult to correct these once poor examples have become set in the mind of the worshipper.

- Liturgy needs to affirm the links formed in the memory which can focus the connections between different aspects of the same word or idea. It also needs to be aware of the way certain words and actions can become attached to tragic or painful events so that they cannot be easily used on general occasions without reference to the loss or hurt.

- Liturgy will recognize that repetition is essential for the retention of material in the memory. It will therefore be cautious about the amount of variable material introduced into a service of worship. The value of repetition will be noted and the constant use of familiar prayers will be maintained.

- In liturgy it will be noted that the first sequence of a section will have major impact on the worshipper. The opening of worship will be constructed with care and each subsequent section contain a strong beginning. In the same way the concluding sequences will be carefully crafted so that the worshipper carries out a memorable ending.

- In written liturgy attention will be paid to the desire by the memory to see a pattern and shape which can be remembered and recognized. The way the words are set out on a page will have a major influence as to how well they are remembered.

- Liturgy will be memorable when it contains a limited number of unique highlights. Too many special points only overload the memory, but there is need for something different and remarkable at significant points.

- Liturgy is dramatic worship and therefore can involve all the five senses, yet too often such actions are described rather than experienced. The Holy Space will have its own fragrance to be smelt, whether these be flowers, polish, or incense. There is the sense of touch with the waters of baptism, the laying on of hands in blessing, Confirmation, or the passing of the peace. There is the taste of the Holy Sacraments, and the tea and biscuits of the post-worship fellowship. There is the sight of the coloured altar cloths, or the seasonal banners, and of the clergy and lay officiants in their robes. The hearing is involved both in listening and responding to the words of the liturgy and the singing of the hymns or songs.

- Memorable liturgy occurs when the general is applied to the particular and the personal. This specially concerns the prayers of intercession and the sermon which will apply the readings to the life of the worshippers. Place and occasion for personal intercession and thanksgiving within the total liturgy often anchors the service of worship for those people who may come under some stress or with a special need.
- Worship will stay memorable over a period of time when it is refreshed with regular reflection, with written material to be read again during the week, and with a clear connection between private prayer and public worship. When worship follows a set sequence, such as the Sundays in Lent and Advent, then each worship occasion can pick up the memories of those in the sequence.
- The memory of worship is retained when set words are repeated regularly, when variable parts such as readings and collects make strong linkages with each other, and when music adds another layer to the memory.
- The sense of 'belonging' in liturgy creates a firm self-identity both for the individual worshipper and the corporate community. Regular contact with people known and identified as one of the group affirms this self-identity.

Chapter 3 – Remembering God in Worship

- The opening of times of prayer and liturgy needs to focus on God rather than on 'me' and 'us'. The worshippers will then see themselves as part of the totality of the divine purpose for all of humanity and of creation.
- Known and familiar words will lead the worshipper into a relationship with God which is ever new while at the same time drawing on the strengths of the past. Psalms and canticles as well as familiar hymns create easy bonding between the worshipper and the Divine presence, and leave spare energy for applying the known to the new situation.
- Liturgical worship permits us to stay in touch with the whole of God's character. For this reason composers of liturgy should be cautious about reducing the breadth of the Great Thanksgiving Prayer, the cycle of readings, or the references in prayer to the various attributes of God. The inclusion of a full creed is also recommended.
- Worship should link us with the whole community of God beyond the particular time and place. Reference to the saints of old and the Church throughout the world should make these links obvious to the worshipper. This will also maintain the links to corporate experience and faith.
- Worship should help us search for fullness in our relationship with, and our knowledge of, God. It will also broaden the way we see the application of our discipleship to the whole of life. It will put the present situation in the context of the past and the future which gives a perspective of realism and hope to the present condition.
- Worship must create new memories of the relationship with God so that this relationship is deepened and kept fresh. Participation in tangible liturgy will best form such new memories.

- The use of the Creed within the regular liturgy will affirm the bonds of corporate memory, recall our own baptism, and be a badge of our identity as a Christian disciple.

Chapter 4 – Remembering our Baptism Through Worship

- The memory of our baptism is not so much of a past event as of a current status. One of the objectives of the Liturgy of Word and Sacrament is to help us recall our status as those baptized into Christ.
- The Liturgy of Baptism should be held regularly in the midst of the congregation so that the Christian community is there to welcome the newly baptized, and at the same time is able to recall their own baptism and the responsibilities of disciples for worship and witness. A service of the renewal of the baptismal covenant should be included in the liturgies of the Easter Octave.
- During the Liturgy of Baptism water should be the prominent symbol and the quantity be sufficient to make this obvious. During the service for the renewal of the baptismal covenant the font should be filled with water, and each person be encouraged to make personal contact with the font of new life. During regular times for liturgical worship fresh water can be available in the font for those entering the church to use with the sign of the cross.
- The links between baptism and communion need to be reaffirmed by word and symbol from time to time. The use of the Paschal candle also provides the link between resurrection and baptism. Likewise the oil used for chrism at a baptism can form a link with the anointing of the sick and with anointing in preparation for dying.
- Those baptized as young children should have regular opportunity to gather at the font for teaching on the various aspects of baptism as they grow in the faith. There may be significant times in their lives when the Church reaffirms the baptismal covenant for such children.

Chapter 5 – Remembering Jesus Christ Through the Liturgy of the Eucharist

- The opening section of the Liturgy of the Eucharist needs to give worshippers an opportunity to recall their relationship with God in Christ, and God's memory of them as Christ's beloved disciples.
- The sequence of repentance and forgiveness should recall Christ's work of salvation and the continuing promise of forgiveness to the penitent.
- The readings from Scripture need to be presented in such a way as to reaffirm the memory of the nature of God and the work of Jesus Christ. The sermon needs to encourage the worshippers to make connections between the words remembered and the new situations they face.
- The recitation of the Creed should be a constant part of the liturgy so that the corporately held faith is reaffirmed and its links to baptism maintained.
- The prayers of intercession which follow a set pattern can link the worshipper

to the work of the Ascended Christ in intercession, and can keep the prayers wide enough to touch the whole of humanity.

- The words of the Peace recall Christ's resurrection and the sense of touch recalls the fellowship of the Spirit of Christ as found within the Christian community.
- The contents of the Great Thanksgiving Prayer maintain the memory of God's activity for the salvation of God's people, and all of humanity, vividly in the minds of the worshippers. The sacramental symbols, through the activity of the Holy Spirit, become the means whereby each worshipper can relive the relationship with Christ, and reform his body in the community of the communicants.
- The Fraction and the Distribution of the Sacrament recall the passion of Christ and the work of salvation with an impact that combines sensory participation with revived memory.
- The affirmation of the Body of Christ and its work at the Blessing and Dismissal recalls the imperative of, and the equipment for, mission. The renewed memory of Christ is carried forth to support the future life and ministry of the communicants.

Chapter 6 – Sustaining Corporate Memory Through Worship

- Worship needs to demonstrate how Scripture, story and encounter are bound together to form our corporate memory of God.
- Corporate rituals through worship are a vital part of sustaining the memory of God's work in Christ for all people.
- Corporate faith and vision is built up through creeds, hymns and songs repeated during worship.
- The sense of corporate identity is affirmed by the regular worship of the community particularly following a cycle of worship appropriate for different occasions. If this does not occur, the corporate memory and its identity fade out.
- Leaders of worship are required to show how the corporate memory is still valid and applies to the current context so that the community can face its new challenges.
- The degree of change and the pace of change within the worship of the Church must not be set so greatly that the corporate memory of worship within society is broken.
- It is the duty of the 'elders' to transmit the sense of common identity which accompanies corporate memory. This applies both to the Church as a community and to society at all levels. The elders are also responsible for passing the corporate story on to the next generations. This will include the identification of key events and the key persons in the story. The honouring of the 'saints' is part of this responsibility. The continual application of the common story to the current context will safeguard the community from lapsing into nostalgia.
- The corporate memory as expressed through worship will sustain 'hope'

within the community in its times of crisis and new opportunities. In the same way the corporate memory needs to keep fresh what the community has learnt from dealing with the consequences of pain and hurt, and to note what factors led to reconciliation and healing.

- Corporate worship should mark significant anniversaries and those times when the leadership changes. This will strengthen the common bonds and build a defence against individualism.
- Community involvement in 'family' rituals must continue to form part of worship for the development of corporate memory. Such occasions must not be seen as private to the inner core of the family. Such occasions include the birth of a child, the wedding of a couple in Holy Marriage, the marking of death with a service of hope and thanksgiving, and any significant events within the community, whether they be of joy or tragedy. The Church needs to reclaim its place on these occasions on behalf of the corporate community and its memory.

Chapter 7 – Mending Memories of Sin and Pain Through Liturgy

- Liturgy needs to present clearly the new data of forgiveness through Christ in the face of the continuing sin and pain of humanity. Such new data is contained in the willingness of God to forgive the sins of those who repent.
- Liturgy needs to declare the new standard for baptized disciples that if they truly confess their sins God will forgive them out of love and a desire for new life in all.
- Liturgy needs to give the worshipper time for reflection about the reality of human sin, and the good news of God's actions for salvation.
- Liturgy can demonstrate through the actions of the worshipping community that reconciliation is the way that this community lives.
- For sinners to accept the possibility of forgiveness, the liturgy has to proclaim the good news of salvation with clarity and through the voice of a trustworthy person. The use of the words of Scripture by a representative presbyter who is respected by the people will fulfill this requirement.
- The words and feelings used in the Rite of Reconciliation must reflect the range of personality preferences that exist in the worshipping community.
- The worshipping community needs to offer an experience of reconciliation and acceptance to the penitent during the liturgy. The words of the liturgy should also be followed up with pastoral support for those who are hurt.
- The joy of forgiveness must be the dominant remembrance in the minds of the worshipper following the Rite of Reconciliation.
- The community and the individual must be supported as alongside the memory of God's forgiveness and healing they retain the warning memory of the consequences of sin.
- The individual Rite of Reconciliation (with counsel) needs to be offered clearly to all who need its sense of forgiveness, freedom, strength and support.

- The reconciliation experienced within the Church needs to be made known within society and to the world family of nations as an essential element in lasting peace. The prayers of intercession during worship are an effective means of this proclamation.

Chapter 8 – Using Aids for Remembering During Liturgy

- Liturgy needs to affirm and name the sense of the sacred in human experience. This sense of the sacred can be attached to the building in which worship takes place. Essential to creating this sense of mystery and awe are the building's attributes of beauty, harmony and a use of space that draws the eye beyond the mundane.
- The associations linked to place will form a solid platform for further experiences of a positive relationship with God in worship. What happens inside a building strongly influences our feelings about that place.
- Buildings set aside for worship create a sense of anticipation of the next experience of the divine. This anticipation can be broken if the experience of worship no longer meets the needs and life context of the worshipper.
- The relationships experienced within a building will colour our feelings about it. The church building and the church people are firmly linked. The liturgy needs to bind both the building and the community together.
- Liturgy needs constantly to affirm the link between the symbols which can convey the holy and the divine activity experienced by the worshipper. Liturgy needs to see that 'Symbols mediate transcendence as language mediates meaning.'[1]
- Liturgy needs to make use of symbols that have universal significance with layers of deep meaning. These include light and darkness, water, fire, food and the natural symbols of nature and growth. To include such symbols in the worship format will allow the worshipper to attach many layers and references to these symbols. As symbols are re-employed so former meanings and associations will be revived. This is especially important on festive occasions of special celebration.
- It is the task of liturgy to keep holy symbols 'alive' by maintaining their sense of mystery and association with divine experience.
- Liturgy needs to highlight the importance of Holy Time for the remembrance of God's activity with God's people. This includes the connection between resurrection and new life with Sunday, and the marking of the festivals of Christ's life and work at various times throughout the year. It also includes the regular remembrance of the saints of their generation.

---

[1] Empereur, James (1987), *Worship – Exploring the Sacred*, p. 44.

Chapter 9 – Balancing Continuity and Change in Worship

- The positive value of structure and continuity in liturgy should be noted as being consistent with the way the brain works best following patterns. Liturgy also needs to reflect the changing circumstances of life of which the brain is aware and to which it looks for a response.
- Liturgy needs to note the triggers by which a change of patterns of behaviour can be facilitated.
- In proposing changes to a set liturgy those responsible need to take into account the factors of age differential, training and educational methodology, personality preferences, and changes in corporate beliefs. The use of options within the liturgy may be necessary to match this diversity.
- Alterations to the liturgy must respond to established needs for clarity and application to changes of context rather than to the 'good ideas' of the composers of liturgy. Practical considerations need to be put alongside theological considerations.
- An appeal to antiquity is not sufficient reason for making changes to established worship patterns. It should not be put forward as an excuse for amendments proposed for other purposes.
- Divisions over liturgical changes can reflect power struggles which may arise from a number of causes. Amendments to the liturgy will only be helpful when all groups respect one another and feel that their point of view has been heard and taken into account.
- Changes in liturgical patterns provide a new opportunity to satisfy the quest for knowledge which is an inherit principle of the brain.
- Any liturgical changes often lessen the ability of society in general to participate in worship. Extra effort will be needed to maintain the links with society during and after liturgical changes.
- The common acceptance of various liturgical forms in the different churches will assist the overall development of liturgy. Opportunities for 'cross fertilization' will benefit all churches.
- The use of sacred music as part of the liturgy highlights the need for both continuity and change. All the factors recorded about changes in liturgy equally apply to the use of music. Therefore the combination of music and words needs further consideration by liturgical experts. Churches may want to hold consultations on this issue as a matter of urgency.

Chapter 10 – Using Imagination in Worship

- Liturgy needs to give worshippers an opportunity to exercise the imaginative function in the brain. This will entail the provision of time for reflection and stimulation as to how to apply parables and metaphors to life situations.
- During worship the imagination can be fired by art, music, poetry and story, and these should form part of the act of worship.
- Liturgy should enable the worshipper to consider the future as well as the past, and the transcendent as well as the immanent. It should also help the

worshipper stay in touch with the present situation and guard against illusion and delusion. Liturgical leaders will safeguard the congregation from deluded interpretations of Scripture and the Spirit's voice.

- Worship should help those attending focus on matters of life-giving concern and avoid trivia. It will assist worshippers to integrate the whole of their lives, and see them as part of God's ultimate purpose.
- Worship should add to the collective knowledge and experience of God within the community. It should also assist those involved in worship to broaden their empathy and sympathy for those in the community for whom they pray. Worship should build up a set of values, a strong corporate faith and a commitment to the common purpose of the community.
- Worship needs to give those attending a foretaste of the breadth of the Christian community, put them in touch with the saints, and see 'over the horizon' to what each person and the whole of creation will be like when the purpose of God is fulfilled.
- Liturgy should help each worshipper develop the tradition of contemplative, ascetic, creative and sacramental prayer.
- Liturgy should recognize the place of the Holy Spirit in the development of the worshipper's ability to be open and receptive to God in worship.
- Liturgy should create a vision of the future which sustains hope. This will include a prophetic vision which expresses the metaphor of the kingdom of God and gives hope for the fulfillment of God's final revelation and purpose.
- Liturgy will speak in the language of poetry as well as prose. It will therefore be liturgy which 'results from the creative interaction between the imaginative vision of the artist and the disciplined energy of tradition'.[2]

---

[2] Avis, Paul (1999), *God and the Creative Imagination*, p. 85.

Bibliography

Alridge, Alan, (1996), 'Slaves to no sect: The Anglican Clergy and Liturgical Change', in Francis, Leslie and Jones, Susan (eds), *Psychological Perspectives on Christian Ministry*, Leominster: Gracewing.

Anglican Church in New Zealand (1989), *A New Zealand Prayer Book/He Karakia Mihinare o Aotearoa*, Auckland and London: Collins [cited as NZPB (1989)].

Atkins, Peter (2001), *Ascension Now – Implications of Christ's Ascension for Today's Church*, Collegeville, MN: The Liturgical Press.

Atkins, Peter (1999), *Worship 2000! – Resources to celebrate the new millennium*, London: HarperCollins.

Avis, Paul (1999), *God and the Creative Imagination*, London and New York: Routledge.

Bal, Micke, Crewe, Jonathan and Spitzer, Leo (eds) (1999), *Acts of Memory: Cultural Recall in the Present*, Hanover, NH and London: Dartmouth College, University Press of New England.

Bathum, Mike (2002), 'Discovering Creative Depths Within', in Culbertson, Philip L. (ed.), *The Spirituality of Men*, Minneapolis, MN: Fortress Press.

Bouyer, Louis (1968), *Eucharist: Theology and Spirituality of the Eucharistic Prayer*, Notre Dame, IN: University of Notre Dame Press.

Bower, Gordon H. and Morrow, Daniel G. (1990), 'Mental Models in narrative comprehension', *Science* 247.

Bradshaw, Paul F. and Hoffman, Lawrence A. (eds) (1996), *Life Cycles In Jewish and Christian Worship*, Notre Dame, IN: University of Notre Dame Press.

Bradshaw, Paul (2002), *The Search for the Origins of Christian Worship*, 2nd edition, London: SPCK.

Brueggemann, Walter (1987), *Hope within History*, Atlanta: John Knox Press.

Buzan, Tony (1993), *The Mind Map Book*, London: BBC Books.

Buzan, Tony (1995), *Use Your Head*, London: BBC Books.

Cairns, David (1967), *In Remembrance of Me – Aspects of the Lord's Supper*, London: Geoffrey Bles.

Calvin, William (1997), *How Brains Think: Evolving Intelligence, Then and Now*, London: Weidenfeld & Nicolson.

Cameron, Averil (2001), 'The Creed', in Conway, Stephen (ed.), *Living the Eucharist*, London: Darton, Longman & Todd.

Chinn, Clark A. and Brewer, William (1998), 'Theories of Knowledge Acquisition', in Fraser, B.J. and Tobin, K.G. (eds), *International Handbook of Science Education*, 97–113, London: Kluwer Academic Publishers.

Conway, Stephen (ed.) (2001), *Living the Eucharist*, London: Darton, Longman & Todd.

Cooey, Paula M. (1994), *Religious Imagination and the Body*, New York and Oxford: Oxford University Press.

Cotter, Jim (1996), *Love Re-membered – Resources for a House Eucharist*, Sheffield: Cairns Publications.

Cullman, O. and Leenhardt, F.J. (1958), *Essays on the Lord's Supper*, London: Lutterworth Press.

Dillistone, F.W. (1986), *The Power of Symbols*, London: SCM Press.

Dix, G. (1945), *The Shape of the Liturgy*, London: A & C Black.

Duit, Reinders and Treagast, David (1998), 'Learning in Science – From Behaviourism Towards Social Reconstruction and Beyond', in Fraser, B.J. and Tobin, K.G. (eds), *International Handbook of Science Education*, 3–25, London: Kluwer Academic Publishers.

Durback, Robert (ed.) (2002), *Henri Nouwen, In My Own Words*, London: Darton, Longman & Todd.

Edelman, Gerald (1992), *Bright Air, Brilliant Fire – On The Matter of the Mind*, London: Penguin Books.

Elliott, Charles (1988), *Signs of Our Times – Prayer and Action to Change the World*, Basingstoke: Marshall Pickering.

Elliott, Charles (1995), *Memory and Salvation*, London: Darton, Longman & Todd.

Elliott, Charles (1999), *Locating the Energy for Change: An Introduction to Appreciative Inquiry*, Winnipeg: International Institute for Sustainable Development.

Empereur, James (1987), *Worship – Exploring the Sacred*, Washington DC: The Pastoral Press.

Eslinger, Richard (1995), *Narrative and Imagination*, Minneapolis, MN: Fortress Press.

Francis, Leslie J. and Atkins, Peter, *Exploring Luke's Gospel* (2000), *Exploring Matthew's Gospel* (2001), *Exploring Mark's Gospel* (2002), London: Mowbray/ Continuum.

Gaster, Theodor (1958), *Passover, Its History and Traditions*, London and New York: Abelard-Schuman.

Green, Garrett (1989), *Imagining God*, San Francisco: Harper and Row.

Harris, Maria (1987), *Teaching and Religious Imagination*, San Francisco: HarperCollins.

Henke, Linda Witte (2001), *Marking Time – Christian Rituals for All Our Days*, Harrisburg, PA: Morehouse Publishing.

Houtman, Cornelius (1996), *Historical Commentary of the Old Testament: Exodus*, Vol. 2, Kampen, The Netherlands: Koh Publishing House.

Krier, Catherine H. (1988), *Symbols for All Seasons*, San Jose, CA: Resource Publications.

La Verdiere, Eugene (1996), *The Eucharist in the New Testament and the Early Church*, Collegeville, MN: The Liturgical Press.

Lasch, Christopher (1991), *The True and Only Heaven – Progress and its Critics*, New York/London: W.W. Norton & Co.

Lathrop, Gordon W. (1993), *Holy Things – A Liturgical Theology*, Minneapolis, MN: Fortress Press.

Lathrop, Gordon W. (1987), 'How Symbols Speak in Liturgy: Central Symbols', *Journal of the Liturgical Conference*, Vol. 1, No. 7, Washington DC.

Lloyd, Trevor (1984), *Introducing Liturgical Change*, Bramcote: Grove Worship Series No. 87, Grove Books.

McIntyre, John (1987), *Faith, Theology and Imagination*, Edinburgh: The Handsel Press.

Mackey, James (ed.) (1986), *Religious Imagination*, Edinburgh: Edinburgh University Press.

Marton, F. (1986), 'Phenomenography – A Research Approach to Investigate Different Understandings of Reality', *Journal of Thought*, Vol. 21, No. 3.

Merton, Thomas (1956, reprinted 1983), *The Living Bread*, Tunbridge Wells: Burns and Oates.

Mitchell, Leonel (1975), *Liturgical Change: How much do we need?*, New York: Seabury Press.

Moriarty, Michael (1996), *The Liturgical Revolution: Prayer Book Revision and Associated Parishes: A Generation of Change in the Episcopal Church*, New York: The Church Hymnal Corporation.

Pfatteicher, Philip H. (1995), *The School of the Church – Worship and Christian Formation*, Valley Forge, PA: Trinity Press International.

Pinker, Steven (1999), *How the Mind Works*, London: Penguin Books.

Platten, Stephen and Pattison, George (1996), *Spirit and Tradition – An Essay on Change*, Norwich: Canterbury Press.

Procter-Smith, Marjorie (1996), 'Contemporary Challenges to Christian Life-Cycle Ritual', in Bradshaw, Paul and Hoffman, Lawrence (eds), *Life Cycles in Jewish and Christian Worship*, Notre Dame, IN and London: University of Notre Dame Press.

Robinson, John (1962), *Honest to God*, London: SCM.

Rosenfield, Israel (1992), *The Strange, Familiar, and Forgotten: An Anatomy of Consciousness*, New York: Knopf.

Segal, J.B. (1963), *The Hebrew Passover*, London: Oxford University Press.

Senge, Peter et al. (1999), *The Dance of Change*, New York: Currency/Doubleday.

Sheldrake, Philip (2001), *Spaces for the Sacred-Place, Memory and Identity*, London: SCM Press.

Stauffer, S. Anita (1999), *Baptism, Rites of Passage and Culture*, Geneva: Lutheran World Federation.

Stevenson, Kenneth (2002), *Do This – The Shape, Style and Meaning of the Eucharist*, Norwich: Canterbury Press.

Stookey, Laurence H. (1982), *Baptism – Christ's Act in the Church*, Nashville: Abingdon Press.

Stookey, Laurence H. (1993), *Eucharist – Christ's Feast with the Church*, Nashville: Abingdon Press.

Stookey, Laurence H. (1996), *Calendar – Christ's Time for the Church*, Nashville: Abingdon Press.

Stringer, Martin D. (1999), *On the Perception of Worship*, Birmingham: University of Birmingham Press.

Swanson, R.N. (ed.) (1999), *Continuity and Change in Christian Worship*, Woodbridge: The Boydell Press.

Thurian, Max (1998), 'The Lima Liturgy', in Best, Thomas and Heller, Dagmar (eds), *Eucharistic Worship in Ecumenical Contexts*, Geneva: WCC Publications.

Tilley, Christopher (1999), *Metaphor and Material Culture*, Oxford: Blackwell.

Torrance, Thomas F. (1969), *Space, Time and Incarnation*, London: Oxford University Press.

Underhill, Evelyn (1936), *Worship*, London: Nisbet & Co.

White, James F. (1999), *The Sacraments in Protestant Practice*, Nashville: Abingdon Press.

Whitehead, A.N. (1928), *Symbolism*, Cambridge: Cambridge University Press.

Willimon, William H. (1980), *Remember Who You Are: Baptism a Model for Christian Life*, Nashville: The Upper Room.

Wren, Brian (2000), *Praying Twice: The Music and Words of Congregational Song*, Louisville: Westminster/John Knox Press.

Young, Robert (1979), *Religious Imagination – God's Gift to Prophets and Preachers*, Philadelphia: Westminster Press.

Index